The Human Constraint

The Coming Shortage of
Managerial Talent

The Human Constraint

The Coming Shortage of Managerial Talent

John B. Miner
Research Professor of Management
Georgia State University

BNA
BOOKS

The Bureau of National Affairs, Inc., Washington, D. C.
1974

Printed in the United States of America
Library of Congress Catalog Card Number 74-76730
International Standard Book Number 0-87179-215-X

Preface

Predicting the future has been a major preoccupation, some would say an obsession, of mankind throughout history. We have had a continuing succession of prophets, soothsayers, and seers, followed in recent years by planners, forecasters, and futurists. It is tempting to dismiss all as equally uncertain; discriminating among predictions in terms of their factual basis is a difficult and time-consuming process. Yet some predictions are merely speculation, while others are solidly grounded in research and analysis.

I would like to believe that my predictions fall in the latter category. In any event they do have the backing of a large amount of research, and they deal with a topic, managerial manpower, which has been the major focus of my work for twenty years. What I say in this book is the product of a great deal of effort and thought. It represents the gradually emerging conclusions of a person who views himself as generally rather conservative, and is certainly not fond of making risky predictions about events in the future.

This book is about the prospect of a massive managerial talent shortage in the United States, and what can be done about it. It is a full-scale presentation of what was said in abbreviated form in an article in the November-December 1973

Harvard Business Review entitled "The Real Crunch in Managerial Manpower." Although the major theme is managerial manpower planning, other topics have emerged as I followed the lead of the subject matter. Among the topics discussed are student activism, social change, the organizational effects of computers, participative management, organization development, organization planning, management development, and business education. In each instance I have tried to treat the subject as objectively as possible, drawing heavily on recent research findings. That my conclusions in these areas often do not jibe with the expressed opinions of other writers is something of which I am well aware, and it is a source of concern to me. But I believe that what I have to say does correctly interpret the available data.

Chapters 2, 3, 4, 9, and 14 contain reports of much of my own research. In the interest of communicating to as wide an audience as possible I have not included any of the statistical analyses. However, my interpretations and discussion are limited to those findings which do meet the conventional criteria for statistical significance. Practically all of the studies have been published in the scientific literature. I have listed in the back of the book those of my publications which deal in greater detail with the topics discussed. The interested reader is referred to these sources for more specific information on methodology, samples, statistical analyses, and the like.

I have been influenced and helped in developing the ideas presented here by a great many people, far too many to mention by name. However, in the early stages of my theorizing and research the contributions of three individuals stand out in particular. One is Professor Silvan S. Tomkins, now of Rutgers University, who was my senior professor at Princeton during both my undergraduate and graduate years. The second is Professor Eli Ginzberg, of Columbia University, who introduced me to the study of manpower problems. The third is William M. Read, of the Atlantic-Richfield Company, through whose efforts

I first began work in the field of management development. To these individuals, and to all the others who have worked with me, and in some cases disagreed with me, over the years since, I express my sincere appreciation.

J.B.M.

Atlanta
January 1974

Contents

Preface   v

List of Exhibits   xv

PART I.   THE NATURE OF THE PROBLEM

Chapter 1   /   The Coming Crunch in Executive Talent   3

The Changing Labor Force   4
Management As A Growth Occupation   8
Declining Motivation to Manage   9

Chapter 2   /   Motivation to Manage and Managerial
Success   13

Aspects of Motivation to Manage   14
When Motivation to Manage Is Lacking   19
Motivation and Success in R & D Management   22
Department Store Managers   23
School Administrators in a Large City   26
What Causes What?   28
An All-American Boy?   31

Chapter 3   /   Motivation to Manage and Wanting to Be a
Manager   33

Why College Students Want to Manage   35

The M. B. A. and D. B. A. Students 37
Managers and University Professors Compared 40
Management Consultants and Managers 41
Student Managers in a Simulated Company 43

Chapter 4 / Change on the Campus 49

Overall Trends: 1960-73 49
Motives That Changed and Motives That Did Not 52
Individual Universities 55
Liberal Arts Students as Potential Managers 58
Graduate Students in Business 59
Managers and Students 61
Managers in Business and Government 64
The Managerial Talent Shortage 67

Chapter 5 / Change in Broad Perspective 71

Julian Rotter's Research on Trust and Control 71
Studies on Authoritarianism 73
Changes in Values 75
The Harvard Business School Research 76
What They Think 78
Attitudes Toward Business and Managing 81
What Do They Want? 84
Company Experience 87
Dimensions of Change 88

Chapter 6 / Student Activism and Protest 91

The Rise of Protest 91
Changing Motives and Activist Behavior 94
Student Power 98
Comparisons With Activists 99
The "Small Minority" View of Activism 101
The New Left versus the Human Constraint 104

Chapter 7 / The Roots of Social Change   107

The Central Role of Authority Relationships   108
Authority, Guilt, and Humanism   109
Disturbed Authority Relationships and Managing   111
Roots of Change: The Evidence From Achievement
     Motivation   113
The Break in Value Transmission   115
The Family Backgrounds of Student Activists   119
Converging Forces   121

PART II. WHAT CAN BE DONE?

Chapter 8 / Managerial Manpower Planning and the Search
          for Strategies   125

Sweeping the Problem Under the Rug   126
Managerial Manpower Planning   128
Developing Strategies   130
Management Appraisal   131
Strategies for Small Businesses and Professional
     Firms   133
The Older Manager and Retirement Policies   134

Chapter 9 / New Sources of Talent   137

Tapping New Sources   139
Aspects of Management Potential   140
Women as Managers?   143
The Supply of Female Talent   144
Minority Groups as a Source of Managerial Talent   150
Internal Search for Management Potential   154
Input Strategies Overall   156

Chapter 10 / The Computer as Manager   159

The Expected Demise of Middle Management   161
Why Is Middle Management Needed?   162

Impact of Technology on Structure   163
Impact of Technology on People   167

Chapter 11 / The Participative Alternative   169

The Need for Control   170
The World of Practice   172
How Good Is Participation?   175
Sources of Misinterpretation   176
The Quality of Participative Decisions   178
Pressures for Centralization   180
Participation as a Strategy   183

Chapter 12 / Organization Development   187

What Is Organization Development?   188
The New Values   190
OD Values and the New Generation   193
Organization Development and the Organization   194
Contraindications to OD   196
The OD Strategy   197

Chapter 13 / Variable Structuring   201

The Specifics of Variable Structuring   202
Retention of Hierarchic Control   207
Project and Matrix Structures   208
Entrepreneurship Through Venture Teams   211

Chapter 14 / Managerial Role-Motivation Training   215

Training Procedures and Content   216
Change in an R & D Department   218
Change Among Business Administration Students   222
Change Among Women   226
Those Who Change and Those Who Do Not   227
The Feasibility of Role-Motivation Training   230

Chapter 15 / Management Development and Education for Managing 233

Compatible Management Development Procedures 233
Training Strategies 237
The Role of the Business School 238
A School of Managing 240

Chapter 16 / The Crunch Reconsidered 243

The Components of a Strategy 243
The Problem for Society 245
Society's Solutions 247

Publications Discussed 249

Publications by the Author Dealing In Greater Detail With the Topics Discussed 259

Index 263

List of Exhibits

Exhibit 1 / Distribution of the Labor Force by Age — 1960 to 1985 5

Exhibit 2 / Six Components of the Motivation to Manage 6

Exhibit 3 / Motivation to Manage at Different Levels of Success in the R & D Department of a Major Oil Company 23

Exhibit 4 / Motivation to Manage at Different Levels of Success in a Department Store 25

Exhibit 5 / Motivation to Manage at Different Levels of Success in a Large City School District 27

Exhibit 6 / Initial Motivation to Manage and Number of Subsequent Promotions in the R & D Department of an Oil Company 28

Exhibit 7 / Initial Motivation to Manage and Rate of Subsequent Promotion in the Marketing Department of an Oil Company 29

Exhibit 8 / Initial Motivation to Manage and Level of Subsequent Performance Rating for Managers Who Separated 30

Exhibit 9 / Motivation to Manage and the Career Choices of Undergraduate Business Students 36

Exhibit 10 / Motivation to Manage and the Career Choices of Graduate Business Students 39

Exhibit 11 / Motivation to Manage of Business Managers With Advanced Degrees and University Professors of Business Administration 41

Exhibit 12 / Motivation to Manage of Business Managers and Management Consultants (Business Specialists) 42

Exhibit 13 / Motivation to Manage and Being Chosen to Manage in a Simulated Business Firm 45

Exhibit 14 / Motivation to Manage of Business Administration Students: 1960-73 51

Exhibit 15 / Motivation to Manage of Business Administration Students at the University of Oregon: 1960-73 56

Exhibit 16 / Motivation to Manage of Business Administration and Liberal Arts Students at the University of Maryland: 1969-73 57

Exhibit 17 / Motivation to Manage of Graduate Business Administration (M.B.A.) Students: 1964-73 60

Exhibit 18 / Comparison of Early and Recent Business Students and Business Managers for Motives That Have Changed 62

Exhibit 19 / Motivation to Manage of Managers in Business and Government 65

Exhibit 20 / Motivation to Manage of Graduate Students Preparing for Managerial Careers in Business and Government (1964-66) 66

Exhibit 21 / Motivation to Manage and Authoritarianism Among College Students 74

Exhibit 22 / Student Self-Perceptions in 1970 as Compared to 1962 77

Exhibit 23 / Attitudes Expressed by College Students 80

Exhibit 24 / Preference . . . for Various Careers and Organizations Among High School Students 83

Exhibit 25 / Differences Between 1962 and 1970 Students in Characteristics of Preferred Companies 85

Exhibit 26 / Approval of Student Activism by Faculty in Various Fields 100

Exhibit 27 / Percent of Students With Very High Managerial Motivation in the Early and Late 1960s 103

Exhibit 28 / Motivation to Manage of Female Managers at Different Levels in a Department Store 144

Exhibit 29 / Motivation to Manage of Male and Female Managers in a Department Store 146

Exhibit 30 / Motivation to Manage of Male and Female Business Administration Majors 148

Exhibit 31 / The Effects of Computers on Clerical and Supervisory Job Size in 23 Insurance Companies 166

Exhibit 32 / Degree of Support for Various Uses of a Participative Approach 174

Exhibit 33 / Number of Lawsuits Filed in Federal District Court by Area 182

Exhibit 34 / Effects of Managerial Role-Motivation Training on Motivation to Manage in an R & D Department 220

Exhibit 35 / Effects of Managerial Role-Motivation Training on Later Success in an R & D Department 221

Exhibit 36 / Effects of Managerial Role-Motivation Training on the Motivation to Manage of Business Administration Students at the University of Oregon 223

Exhibit 37 / Results of a Comparison Study to See if Changes Comparable to Those With Role-Motivation Training Occur in Other Courses 224

Exhibit 38 / Results of Studies to Determine if Changes in Motivation to Manage are Retained 225

Exhibit 39 / Effects of Managerial Role-Motivation Training on the Motivation to Manage of Female College Students 227

Exhibit 40 / Changes in Motivation to Manage Resulting From Role-Motivation Training in People of Different Temperaments 229

Exhibit 41 / Extent to Which Managers In India Were Active in Stimulating Business Growth and New Business Ventures (Entrepreneurship) as Related to Achievement Motivation Training 236

Part 1

The Nature of
the Problem

1

The Coming Crunch
in Executive Talent

The theme of this book is that the United States is headed for a shortage of executive talent so severe that if something is not done about it, the country's economic growth could well come to a standstill. Several factors contributing to this situation were outlined in an article written by Arch Patton of McKinsey and Company in 1967. Patton wrote, ". . . a no holds barred scramble for executive talent . . . will develop in the next few years. Indeed, the demand for this increasingly rare commodity could reach such boom proportions by 1975 that even the best-managed companies, which have executive talent in consider-able depth today, would be unfavorably affected."

The four factors entering into Patton's prediction were as follows:

- The low birthrate of the 1930s.
- The unprecedented expansion in the size of the average corporation in recent years.
- The increasing complexity of the management process.
- The burgeoning demand for executive talents outside industry — notably in government and education.

Important as these factors are, a fifth consideration that was not yet evident in 1967 now appears to be of even greater importance:

• The change in student attitudes and motivation that first clearly manifested itself on college campuses in the mid-1960s.

The fact is that this country has lost one of its most vital resources, its motivation to manage, at least in its younger generation. If solutions to this problem, and to the problems posed by Arch Patton, are not found, many of the country's large organizations will founder leaderless before long. My purpose in writing this book is to make as many people as possible aware of these problems, of which I first became fully aware as a result of my own research, and to point out what can be done to mobilize action focused on their solution before it is too late.

The Changing Labor Force

There is no question that the low birth rate during the Depression years of the 1930s coupled with the high rate after World War II has produced a dislocation in the labor force. U.S. government figures and projections indicate that the age group 35—54, from which most corporate managers come, has been shrinking relative to the rest of the labor force, and that it will shrink more. In 1960 this age cohort represented 43 percent of the labor force. By 1968 it was down to 41 percent and the anticipated figure for 1975 is 37 percent. A low point of 35 percent is projected for 1980, but the increase by 1985 will be only back to 37 percent, and at that point the pool from which older, more experienced managers must be drawn will be even lower than in 1980. Thus with a steadily increasing total labor force the country is faced for at least the next fifteen years with depressed proportions in the age groups from which managers are drawn.

As Professor Eric Vetter, of Tulane University, has noted, the problem posed by this relative deficit in the managerial age group has been compounded by the manpower policies followed by many companies during the Depression and World War II. During the 1930s most firms did little to hire and develop managerial talent; they were too concerned with immediate survival. Manpower shortages during the war years perpetuated this situation for another five years. Thus for some fifteen years little was done to feed new talent into managerial promo-

---

EXHIBIT 1
Distribution of the Labor Force by Age
1960 - 1985

Age Group	Percent of Labor Force				
	1960	1968	1975	1980	1985
16−24	18	22	23	23	21
25−34	21	20	24	26	27
35−44	23	21	18	19	22
45−54	20	20	19	16	15
55−64	13	13	13	13	12
65 and over	5	4	3	3	3
Total size of the labor force (in millions)	72	82	93	101	107

Adapted from an article by Sophia Travis in the May 1970 issue of *Monthly Labor Review*.

---

tion channels and to develop future executives. To some extent the consequences of this situation are still with us, and will be for another ten to fifteen years.

Data on the composition of the labor force suggest that a solution might be found in moving young people up to managerial responsibilities more rapidly, thus tapping the rapidly expanding 25−34 age group. In spite of the risks involved, this clearly would eliminate considerations related to the changing age distribution of the labor force. On the other hand, it runs squarely into the problems created by the declining motivation to manage of the younger generation.

EXHIBIT 2

Six Components of the Motivation to Manage

1. *Favorable attitude toward those in positions of authority, such as superiors.* Managers typically are expected to behave in ways which do not provoke negative reactions from their superiors; ideally they will elicit positive responses. A manager must be in a position to represent his group upward in the organization and to obtain support for his actions at higher levels. This requires a good relationship between the individual and superiors. It follows that a manager should have a generally positive attitude toward those holding positions of authority over him, if he is to meet this particular job requirement.

2. *Desire to engage in competition, especially with peers.* There is, at least insofar as peers are concerned, a strong competitive element built into managerial work. Behavior of this kind might not be necessary if the job existed independent of its organizational context, but this is not the case. A manager must compete for the available rewards, both for himself and for his group. If he does not, he may lose ground as he and his operation are relegated to lower and lower status levels. Rapid promotion is certainly very improbable without competitive behavior. Thus managers must characteristically strive to win, for themselves and their groups, and accept such challenges as other managers at a comparable level may offer. On occasion the challenge may come from below, even from among one's own subordinates. In order to meet this job requirement a person should be favorably disposed toward engaging in competition.

3. *Desire to assert oneself and take charge.* There is a marked parallel between the requirements of the managerial role and the traditional assertive demands of the masculine role as it is defined in our society. Although the behaviors expected of a father and those expected of a manager are by no means identical, there are many similarities. Both are supposed to take charge, to make decisions, to take such disciplinary action as may be necessary, and to protect the other members of their group. Thus, one of the more common role requirements of the managerial job is that the incumbent behave in an assertive, masculine manner. Even when women are appointed to managerial positions they are expected to be able to take charge, at least during the hours spent in the work situation. It follows that a desire to meet require-

ments for assertiveness should generally lead to success in meeting certain requirements of the managerial job as well.

4. *Desire to exercise power and authority over others, particularly subordinates.* This is the requirement that a manager must exercise power over his subordinates and direct their behavior in a manner consistent with organizational, and presumably his own, objectives. He must tell others what to do when this becomes necessary, and enforce his words through appropriate use of positive and negative sanctions. The individual who finds such behavior difficult and emotionally disturbing, who does not wish to impose his wishes on others, or who believes it wrong to do so, would not be expected to meet this particular job requirement.

5. *Desire to behave in a distinctive and different way, which involves standing out from the crowd.* The managerial job tends to require a person to behave in ways differing in a number of respects from the behavior of others in the same face-to-face group. An incumbent must in this sense stand out from his group and assume a position of high visibility. He cannot use the actions of the people with whom he is most frequently associated, his subordinates, as a guide for his own behavior as a manager. Rather he must deviate from the immediate group and do things that will inevitably invite attention, discussion, and perhaps criticism from those reporting to him. The managerial job requires that an individual assume a position of considerable importance insofar as the motives and emotions of other people are concerned. When this prospect is viewed as unattractive, when the idea of standing out from the group, of behaving in a different manner, and of being highly visible elicits feelings of unpleasantness, then behavior appropriate to the job will occur much less often than would otherwise be the case.

6. *Sense of responsibility in carrying out the numerous routine duties associated with managerial work.* The managerial job requires getting the work out and keeping on top of routine demands. The things that have to be done must actually be done. They range from constructing budget estimates to serving on committees, to talking on the telephone, to filling out employee rating forms and salary-change recommendations. There are administrative requirements of this kind in all managerial work, although the specific activities will vary somewhat from one situation to another. To meet these requirements a manager must at least be willing to face this type of routine, and ideally he should gain some satisfaction from it.

Management As A Growth Occupation

The predictions dealing with future managerial manpower indicate not only a declining supply, but an increasing demand. Projections developed by the National Planning Association and reported by Leonard Lecht specify salaried managers as one of thirty-two high-growth occupations. The demand for managers is expected to exceed that for accountants, lawyers, teachers, and the self-employed; it should be roughly equal to that for architects, dentists, scientists, and physicians. In the past twelve years the demand for managers has approximately doubled; it is expected to rise at a similar rate in the future.

Arch Patton noted the increasing complexity of the managerial process, a point with which few who have actually managed over the past decade would quarrel. There appears to be not only a need for more managers, but for better ones. It is also true that there is a growing demand for managers outside the business world, although there is some reason to believe that the nonbusiness sector has often made do in the past with a lesser level of management talent, substituting professional for managerial competence wherever possible. Government and education have suffered from a lack of managerial motivation for some time already.

Yet with the growth in size of these organizations, managerial effectiveness is becoming increasingly a necessity. Government is the fastest growing among the major industry divisions used by the Labor Department in its analysis of employment figures. The number of new government employees projected for the twenty years from 1960 to 1980 far exceeds the number of new employees anticipated in manufacturing and in wholesale and retail trade, for example. Given this situation, it does seem likely that nonbusiness organizations will come increasingly to compete with business for scarce supplies of managerial talent in the years ahead.

Declining Motivation to Manage

Probably more important than any other factor in influencing managerial manpower supplies is the availability of motivation to manage. The significance of this factor and the reason for anticipating even more drastic managerial talent shortages than Arch Patton predicted become evident in the light of the following facts:

    1. Motivation to manage and its constituent attitudes and motives are particularly likely to contribute to —
       a. the choice of a managerial career
       b. success in a managerial position at any level
       c. rapid promotion up the managerial ladder.
    2. These attitudes and motives typically have been at a high level among business managers.
    3. There has been a marked decline in the strength of motivation to manage and of the majority of its constituent attitudes and motives among the college students who would be expected to provide the country with needed managerial talent in the future.

The timing of the change on campus has been such that I do not anticipate the effects of declining motivation to manage to be much in evidence in the business world before the late 1970s. This contrasts with Arch Patton's prediction of major managerial manpower shortages by 1975. On the other hand the low point in the size of the 35 − 54 age group does not occur until 1980. These considerations raise a question as to exactly when the executive talent crunch can be expected to begin. Has it begun already?

An article by George Berkwitt in the February 1973 issue of *Dun's* indicates that some companies have begun to feel the pinch. Berkwitt makes such statements as the following:

    • "From the surplus of just a year ago suddenly there are not enough good managers to go around."

- "Many recruiters report their business is up 30% to 40% over last year."
- "Many personnel men believe that the real crunch will occur later this year."

It is evident that these statements reflect some real problems in filling management positions in certain companies. On the other hand, there is no reason to believe that the shortage would hit all companies at once. Differences in growth rates, retirements, managerial turnover, and most particularly the extent to which a company has developed and stockpiled managerial talent in the past can certainly be expected to exert an influence on the timing of the crunch in a particular situation.

An analysis presented by John Perham, also of *Dun's*, indicates clearly that there are major differences among companies insofar as their current executive talent positions are concerned, and also with regard to their capacity to ward off shortages in the future. Some firms have done a much better job of developing and retaining competent managers than others; often there are special areas of the business where managerial manpower has been developed in particularly great depth. Thus, Exxon has considerable strength among staff managers, Revlon in marketing, IBM among its women managers, General Electric in the financial area, Norton Company among its international managers, Gulf and Western in acquisitions and planning, ITT in financial controls, Textron in general management, Johnson & Johnson in manufacturing, and so on. Companies such as these may not experience managerial talent shortages nearly as soon as others whose efforts at development have been less effective.

Thus, although some firms already are experiencing the crunch, others may not reach the same point until the early 1980s. In fact, some may never reach it if they act now to deal with the problem. The tools either to reverse the motivational changes or to adapt to them are available. Yet in the normal course of events few companies can be expected to make use of them. Unless companies inform themselves about the causes of the problem, corrective action is not likely to be sufficiently on target to do much good. However, with sufficient warning and adequate attention to developing appropriate strategies, a company can ward off the human constraint and avoid the consequences of a lack of managerial talent. Those companies that do not act will almost certainly be forced to curtail expansion and may well have to reduce their operations; the alternative is to experience the effects of widespread managerial incompetence.

2

Motivation to Manage and Managerial Success

Several years ago Marvin Bower, then managing director of the international management consulting firm McKinsey & Company, wrote a book called *The Will to Manage*. In it he sets forth his view of this crucial ingredient in the success of an individual manager, and of the company managed. The will to manage is not the same thing as the will to succeed, yet it is ". . . an essential forerunner of outstanding, long-term success for companies of more than 300 employees." This determination to manage means that managers "will take steps to control the business instead of letting it control them." Bower also notes that ". . . the primary deterrent to developing a stronger will to manage is the natural reluctance of most managers to discipline their subordinates or to injure their feelings."

What Bower calls the *will to manage* I have called the *motivation to manage*. What Bower concludes on the basis of long experience as a consultant to major corporations, and as a manager in his own right, I conclude on the basis of extensive research: To manage well a person has to want to manage; he has to really "love" it.

Bower devotes much of his book to discussing what he calls the systems approach — the way that a person with the will to manage actually does his job. He does not explore the question of the personality makeup, or motivational dynamics, of the person with this will to manage, which has been my major concern. Much of my work has been aimed at identifying the personality characteristics of people who have a strong desire to manage, and at learning how these characteristics contribute to managerial success. What makes such a person tick?

Aspects of Motivation to Manage

An individual with a strong motivation to manage likes to compete, and he likes to exercise power or authority. He is favorably disposed to his superiors and to people in positions of status and authority generally. He wants to be in a distinctive position, and he has a strong sense of responsibility. He enjoys expressing a kind of assertiveness that is often associated with masculinity.

These are all aspects of motivation to manage. Yet people with strong motivation to manage are not all alike. Some enjoy managing through one combination of these characteristics; others through another. Very few experience satisfaction in all aspects of the managerial role when they perform the work of managers. This diversity is evident in the following personality evaluations. All these evaluations are of individuals in sales management positions; each exhibits a strong overall motivation to manage, but the thumbnail sketches provided by professional psychologists depict quite different people.

1. Mr. Fielder clearly enjoys managerial work, and there is considerable reason to believe that he can be very effective in it. He is a very competitive person who wants to get ahead and who will face almost any challenge to achieve this goal. He is not one to be easily discouraged. In fact, competitive situations tend to key him up, with the result that he can be expected to

perform at his best under a certain amount of pressure.

Perhaps consonant with his ambition is a certain amount of aggressiveness which could get him into trouble under some circumstances. In his present work, however, this appears to be something of an asset.

Finally, Mr. Fielder exhibits considerable interest in standing out from his subordinate group. He likes to be an object of attention and does not become anxious at such times. In this sense he can be considered highly competent in dealing with social situations, even those which might present real difficulties to most other people.

Mr. Fielder could be expected to perform very effectively at higher levels should an opportunity for promotion present itself.

2. Mr. Henline exhibits a number of motives which are often associated with managerial success, yet certain problems are in evidence as well. Although capable of dealing effectively with his present position, Mr. Henline has not yet reached his full potential as a manager. The major difficulty is that he is more a doer than a director of the work of others.

Mr. Henline enjoys situations where he can assume an active, take-charge role. He likes to initiate for others, but he tends to achieve this more by setting an example than by telling his subordinates what he wants them to do.

Decisions come easily to him. He is not afraid to fail and thus will take risks when appropriate. Accordingly, one would expect him to have a well-organized operation. Delays will not occur because of a bottleneck in his office. Mr. Henline will work hard and long to be sure things keep moving.

The prospects for advancement and career success appear to be above average. If Mr. Henline can develop a more forceful approach to the leadership process, his prospects should be even more favorable.

3. Mr. Beaton reveals very strong motivation to perform

nearly all aspects of the managerial job. He likes to take charge, is assertive, and has no difficulty bringing himself to make demands on the time of others when this is essential to his work. He enjoys directing the activities of his subordinates and feels it is appropriate that he should tell them what to do. Forceful and direct, he is the kind of person who sees that things get done.

The only area where Mr. Beaton appears to experience difficulty is with regard to certain types of competitive situations. This is not meant to imply a lack of ambition and drive. To the contrary, Mr. Beaton wants very much to get ahead and face new challenges. But he finds it very difficult to handle the process of evaluation by superiors. He does not like to be judged, or to find himself in a situation where he is being closely watched. At such times he is likely to become anxious and perform less effectively.

In spite of this one negative point, Mr. Beaton gives every indication that he possesses outstanding potential for advancement to higher levels. A major barrier might be the necessity of working under a man who made him feel constantly on trial over an extended period of time.

4. Mr. Tanneman thoroughly enjoys managerial work and is strongly motivated to meet the challenges it presents. He has an unusually favorable attitude toward authority figures, so much so that he can become rather unpopular among his fellow managers at times. Yet the result will also be a relatively good working relationship with his superiors.

Insofar as his subordinates are concerned, Mr. Tanneman appears to be quite effective. He enjoys directing others, can be forceful, and will push hard for results, especially if his superiors indicate that is what they want. He may not always be popular, but he is not afraid to tell others what they are to do.

The only negative factor in the motivational picture is a tendency to overlook, or perhaps even avoid, some routine detail work. Mr. Tanneman likes to make decisions and deal with important problems. He wants to impress his superiors and does what he thinks will accomplish this aim. The result is some tendency to neglect those aspects of his work which he considers unimportant.

The prospects for promotion to higher levels of responsibility seem good.

5. Mr. Kretzing has the personality to be a very effective manager. He enjoys assuming a position of leadership and appears to be quite competent in this role. A rather forceful person, he says what he thinks. His subordinates should have little difficulty determining where he stands. He would be expected to exercise considerable control over his operation and to have it well organized. Things should move along smoothly with few hitches. Mr. Kretzing is the type of person who will get the work out as required, and he expects the same of others.

Furthermore, he enjoys making decisions, and seems to have the intellectual equipment and the analytical bent required to do so effectively. He can be counted on to reach for decisions of a broader scope should the opportunity present itself. In this, and other regards as well, he appears to possess the characteristics needed for movement to positions of greater responsibility.

6. Mr. White is very highly motivated relative to the demands of managerial work. His attitude toward superiors is extremely favorable. He respects them and is able to work effectively with them in carrying out his duties.

In dealing with his subordinates, Mr. White tends to be quite directive, and does not hesitate to indicate what he wants done. There is reason to believe, however, that he is not always successful in his efforts to get others to follow his lead. He may push too hard on occasion and thus arouse some resentment. At present he is rather concerned about himself in this regard, and has some serious doubts about the more forceful approach. Yet he likes to exercise power and to stand out from his subordinates, to be visible and at the center of attention. And he is generally skillful in this role. His problems should diminish with greater experience.

When we add to these factors a strong desire to get the work out and keep things moving, there seems little reason to believe that Mr. White will not have an outstanding career. Although not always successful in the past, he seems to have really found himself in managerial work. His potential for advancement appears to be very good.

7. Mr. Glotfelty gives every indication of experiencing great satisfaction in managerial work. He wants very much to be at the center of things and to stand out. It is not so much that he is extremely ambitious as that he enjoys a role in which he makes a difference in the lives of the people around him, in which he can have some impact and exercise some power. In this sense he has a very real thirst for life.

He likes to direct others, especially in a group situation. He can be firm and confident under such circumstances. Certainly he is not one to lose himself in the group. Both his superiors and his subordinates are likely to be very much aware that he is around. He will call frequent meetings of his subordinates, and he will use these meetings to give rather specific directives, not to engage in participative types of decision making.

Mr. Glotfelty should have a long and very satisfying career in management ahead of him. He could attain quite high levels.

The men described in these sketches are people whose motives consistently add up to a strong desire to manage, even though the specific motives that contribute most to the total pattern vary considerably. By way of contrast, we can examine what psychologists have to say about several managers who are not really attracted to managerial work.

When Motivation to Manage Is Lacking

The personality descriptions which follow also derive from psychological methods of analysis and involve sales managers. In these cases, however, motivation to manage is not strong. In fact there is a tendency to pull away from and to avoid many of the things that people who love managing plunge into headlong.

8. Mr. Riordan performs his work not out of any great love for the job, but rather because of a very strong sense of duty. The result is that he is able to compensate at least partially for what would otherwise be a rather strikingly negative motivational pattern. Certainly he is able to force himself to get a good part of his job done. Yet he would prefer to let problems slide and hopefully solve themselves. At best he gets some decisions made and his basic, routine duties performed.

The problem is that Mr. Riordan has a basic and deep-seated dislike of competition. It is unpleasant and upsetting to him, and he will grasp at almost any excuse to avoid it. He becomes anxious under the pressure of competitive endeavor, which covers much that is included in his job, and in spite of his efforts to overcome these feelings, his performance suffers.

Mr. Riordan is not a very active person. He would prefer to remain passive, to be influenced by others rather than to exert influence on them. Because of this lack of drive, potential for advancement would seem to be rather low.

9. Mr. Elwell does not give evidence of developing into a particularly strong manager. He is an extremely cautious individual who likes to think things through in great detail before acting. The result can be that rather frequently he never gets around to acting at all.

He would like not to commit himself on anything, unless it is absolutely essential. It is very difficult to obtain his opinion, even on matters of considerable importance to the performance of his job. In particular, he would like to avoid expressing himself in writing. To do so might result in his being "pinned down" on something at a later date. Thus, his paperwork can be inordinately delayed on occasion, as he attempts to think through related problems with a view to avoiding anything that could hurt him.

Because he is so extremely careful and finds it so difficult to take risks, Mr. Elwell would not seem to be a good prospect for higher levels of responsibility.

10. Mr. Butterfield seems to be interested in just about everything but his management position. He has developed the fiction that he is somehow superior to his work. As a result he appears to have little dedication to the job and is not willing to give what is required to perform effectively. In an occupational sense, at least, he has very limited drive and ambition. He is in no sense competitive.

Mr. Butterfield does, however, enjoy telling others what to do. He is quite willing to direct the activities of his subordinates and can in fact become somewhat dogmatic at times. Unfortunately, his lack of interest in his work restricts his efforts at followup. The result can be considerable in regard to direction of others, but very little effort spent to see that things are actually done.

Basically, this man does not like the managerial job, but because of his rather dominant tendencies has gravitated to it. There seems a good chance that he will eventually find some other vocation. He will fail if promoted.

11. Mr. Mack does not come through as a strong manager. He does not see himself as having much in common with higher levels of management in the company, nor does he really expect to have his efforts recognized in any tangible way by his superiors.

In a sense Mr. Mack considers himself something of a chronic loser, at least within the occupational sphere. Basically, he wants to defend himself and maintain his current level of accomplishment, although he is not at all sure this is possible. He gives no evidence of a desire to conquer new fields. He does not want to assert himself in any way, for fear he might "rock the boat." There is considerable evidence to indicate that his primary desire is to keep away from his superiors, and maintain sufficient silence so that he will not be noticed. Perhaps then others will not find out about his limitations.

Mr. Mack is not one to impose his wishes on others or to tell them what to do. He is rather afraid that they might react negatively and create some unpleasantness. Thus, he is more of a follower than a leader. Furthermore, he is not a very conscientious manager. Routine duties may be overlooked and put off. It may be that Mr. Mack will be unable to maintain his current position, as he fears.

12. Mr. Yates exhibits certain deficiencies in his motivation to perform managerial work which make it unlikely that he will ever be an entirely satisfactory manager. His greatest strength is a generally positive attitude toward those in positions of authority over him, which manifests itself in the belief that his superiors are overburdened and do not receive the rewards they deserve. This attitude may lead somewhat insecure superiors to overvalue his contribution to the company.

This positive factor is, however, outweighed by several negatives. Mr. Yates does not like competitive situations. In fact, he tends to be rather cynical about competitive endeavor as a whole, suggesting that he does not really expect to win out, especially in the occupational sphere. There is also a generally avoidant attitude toward activities which require a "take charge," self-assertive demeanor. Such activities may elicit considerable anxiety, and Mr. Yates exhibits a marked tendency to avoid the unpleasant, and even to blame others for his shortcomings in this regard.

The general impression is of a man who, though likeable, may not get much done. Potential for promotion is limited.

Motivation and Success in R & D Management

Practical experience and observation indicate that the will or motivation to manage makes a great deal of difference in managerial success. The thumbnail psychological evaluations assume that this is the case. But how do we really know? The answer to that question can only come from actual study. At the very least, managers with varying amounts of managerial motivation must be compared to see if strong motivation goes with success and weak motivation with failure.

Evidence obtained from a group of R & D managers in one of the major oil companies is positive on this point. Using a set of psychological scales to determine the level of motivation to manage, I found that high motivation is much more prevalent in the upper levels of department management than at the lower levels. The most pronounced difference is in the desire to compete. The managers who have made it to the top are very competitive people. This level of competitive drive is less common among those who have not as yet moved out of first-level supervision.

Success is not merely a matter of promotion, however; it also involves doing a good job in the present managerial position. Here the best index of what a company really thinks of a manager is provided by a formal management appraisal process. The way this process is carried out in the oil company is best described by quoting from the firm's management personnel inventory and development plan:

"The technique of appraisal consists of two or three people of higher management levels than the man being appraised, who know his work and have some responsibility for it, sitting down and discussing his present performance and future possibilities. The appraisal panel normally includes the appraisee's immediate superior, the latter's superior, and a representative of the Industrial Relations Department. It may under some circumstances include someone outside the department with whom the appraisee has business contacts."

Out of these discussions come two ratings. One deals with performance on the present job and ranges from outstanding to unsatisfactory. The other deals with advancement potential and ranges from outstanding to "replacement needed."

When the strength of motivation to manage is compared against these ratings, the results are positive. Managers who are rated outstanding either on present performance or in potential to move up are in fact more likely to possess motivation to manage than those rated at the lower ends of these two scales.

EXHIBIT 3
Motivation to Manage at Different Levels of
Success in the R & D Department of
a Major Oil Company

	Lower Management	Middle Management	Upper Management
High Motivation	18 (46%)	18 (62%)	22 (69%)
Low Motivation	21 (54%)	11 (38%)	10 (31%)
	Poor Performers	Good Performers	Outstanding Performers
High Motivation	4 (40%)	30 (59%)	12 (60%)
Low Motivation	6 (60%)	21 (41%)	8 (40%)
	Limited Potential	Good Potential	Outstanding Potential
High Motivation	11 (44%)	13 (62%)	25 (71%)
Low Motivation	14 (56%)	8 (38%)	10 (29%)

Department Store Managers

A second opportunity to test the concept of managerial motivation involved a management development program conducted for a department store located in a small city in Oregon. The program itself focused around a business game. We used the managerial motivation scales to see if experience with the game might help to improve motivation. It did not, but as a byproduct we did have an opportunity to find out about the relationship between motivation to manage and success in a very different kind of business enterprise.

As in the oil company, the managers at higher levels in the department store are more likely to possess motivation to manage than the selling supervisors, who devote most of their time to customer sales, and supervise only when higher level managers are not available. In this case, however, a greater variety of aspects of motivation to manage is involved. The department store managers are not only strong competitors; they also want to wield power and they want to be in a distinctive position. These motives combine with a strong sense of responsibility to produce one of the most impressive groups of managers I know.

Management appraisals in the store are made on a variety of factors by a single individual, the store manager. In general, approaches of this kind do not have a great deal to recommend them. The judgment of one person is always somewhat suspect, and particularly so when he must rate a large number of people on a great variety of aspects of performance. Nevertheless, the people rated high by the store manager do show high motivation to manage.

A problem arises, however, because the members of the store's management group who are considered the poorer performers also often exhibit strong motivation to manage. This is not what one might expect. The phenomenon is most pronounced in the case of the cooperation ratings. When the store manager describes a person in terms such as "gives *complete* cooperation and *extends* himself to assist others," the strength of motivation to manage is likely to be much higher than when the second category, "cooperates *willingly* and *gets along* with

EXHIBIT 4
Motivation to Manage at Different Levels
of Success in a Department Store

	Selling Supervisors	Assistant Managers	Department Managers
High Motivation	11 (33%)	8 (47%)	14 (70%)
Low Motivation	22 (67%)	9 (53%)	6 (30%)

	Less Cooperative Performers	Cooperative Performers	Very Cooperative Performers
High Motivation	8 (67%)	8 (29%)	16 (57%)
Low Motivation	4 (33%)	20 (71%)	12 (43%)

	Limited Potential	Good Potential	Outstanding Potential
High Motivation	7 (35%)	12 (43%)	13 (65%)
Low Motivation	13 (65%)	16 (57%)	7 (35%)

others," is selected. But further down the scale, among those described by statements such as "cooperates to a *satisfactory degree, but lacks enthusiasm,*" and "cooperates *under pressure, but must be encouraged to do so by a superior,*" strong motivation is once again in evidence.

Investigation of this situation reveals something about the tenacity with which motivation to manage may be held. If a person with strong motives of this kind is stopped from moving on to greater managerial challenges by virtue of promotional blocks within the company and the absence of opportunity outside it, the motivational pattern does not give way. But what before was the manager's greatest asset, the source of his drive, success, and satisfaction in work, becomes a liability. He pushes too hard and comes to be viewed as increasingly uncooperative, because he cannot accept the real obstacles in his path. The data from the department store teach us that strong motivation to manage needs a world of opportunity and growth in order to prosper. In a truly stagnant environment, it is less likely to wither than to become a force for failure. A company that cannot provide a climate which nurtures the will to manage would do well not to attract people who have this motivation in the first place.

School Administrators in a Large City

Motivation to manage is related to success in organizations as diverse as a large integrated oil company and a retail store, but both are part of the free enterprise system and of the profit-making sector. What about something as different from the business world as a large city public school district?

The answer is much the same. In the schools in Portland, Ore., there is no evidence that the top-level administrators have any more motivation to manage than the low-level elementary school teaching-principals, but there is every reason to believe they should, and that the district would run better if they did.

The basis for this conclusion is an analysis using appraisal data. In this case the rating form uses items that are often different from those that would be included for a business firm. The six items which are combined to get an overall evaluation of performance are:

1. *Performance in relation to subordinates* — ability to elicit effective work from his or her subordinates.

2. *Performance in relation to community* — ability to draw on the resources of the community and its representatives in a way which facilitates the attainment of educational objectives.

3. *Performance in relation to students* — ability to develop and implement policies, rules, and procedures, with reference to students, which contribute to student learning.

4. *Effect on attitudes of subordinates* — ability to create and maintain high levels of satisfaction among subordinates and to keep dissension to a minimum.

5. *Effect on attitudes in the community* — ability to deal with the community and its representatives in a way which fosters a

favorable public feeling toward the school system and minimizes overt conflict between the schools and the community.

6. *Effect on attitudes of the students* — ability to develop and implement policies, rules, and procedures, with reference to students, which lead to student satisfaction and a generally favorable feeling toward school.

EXHIBIT 5
*Motivation to Manage at Different Levels
of Success in a Large City
School District*

	Poor Performers	Good Performers	Outstanding Performers
High Motivation	6 (27%)	10 (50%)	14 (67%)
Low Motivation	16 (73%)	10 (50%)	7 (33%)

	Limited Potential	Good Potential	Outstanding Potential
High Motivation	7 (33%)	10 (48%)	13 (62%)
Low Motivation	14 (67%)	11 (52%)	8 (38%)

When administrators are rated on these questions, those who come out at the top are much more likely to have high motivation to manage than those whom their superiors consider only satisfactory at best. The same holds for the potential-for-advancement ratings. In spite of major differences in jobs, the motivational bases for managerial talent are much the same in extremely varied organizations. Thus, in the school district the high-rated administrators are competitive, enjoy occupying a distinctive position, are assertive, and have very favorable attitudes toward superiors. A person with these motivational characteristics would have a good chance for success in most business firms as well.

What Causes What?

All these analyses — in the oil company, the department store, and the school district — leave one major question unanswered. The crucial feature of the will to manage is that motives of this kind *cause* managers to act in ways that make them and their companies successful. But when the level of motivation and the level of success are measured at about the same point in a person's career, it is impossible to say what causes what. It is important to know that high motivation occurs in conjunction with success and that low motivation is associated with failure, but knowing this makes it important to learn more.

The really important question is whether managers who have high motivation to manage are increasingly successful over time, and whether those whose motivation is weak subsequently fail. Only with this kind of analysis is it possible to say that motivation to manage *causes* success. If people with intense determination to manage move on to outstanding managerial

---

EXHIBIT 6
*Initial Motivation to Manage and Number of Subsequent
Promotions in the R & D Department of
an Oil Company*

Motivation to Manage	No Promotions	One Promotion	Two or More Promotions
High Motivation	3 (25%)	6 (38%)	15 (71%)
Low Motivation	9 (75%)	10 (62%)	6 (29%)
Favorable Attitude Toward Authority			
High Motivation	3 (25%)	5 (31%)	15 (71%)
Low Motivation	9 (75%)	11 (69%)	6 (29%)
Desire for a Distinctive Position			
High Motivation	3 (25%)	5 (31%)	11 (52%)
Low Motivation	9 (75%)	11 (69%)	10 (48%)

accomplishment, it is hardly possible to say that success produced the motivation; the motivation was already there in the first place, and must have produced the success.

I have conducted several analyses of this type in the R & D and Marketing Departments of a major oil company. In the first case, initial differences in motivation to manage were studied in relation to the number of promotions received during the next five years following the motivation measurement. In the second study, promotion rates were analyzed for a period of from three to five years depending on the individual involved. Within the R & D Department, the men were already at the management level when their motivation was initially determined. Within the Marketing Department, the majority started as salesmen, ready to move up into management, but not yet actually there.

EXHIBIT 7
Initial Motivation to Manage and Rate of
Subsequent Promotion in the Marketing
Department of an Oil Company

Motivation to Manage	No Promotions	Slow Promotion Rate	Fast Promotion Rate
High Motivation	13 (32%)	14 (64%)	16 (89%)
Low Motivation	28 (68%)	8 (36%)	2 (11%)
Favorable Attitude Toward Authority			
High Motivation	20 (49%)	16 (73%)	15 (83%)
Low Motivation	21 (51%)	6 (27%)	3 (17%)
Desire to Compete			
High Motivation	7 (17%)	13 (59%)	11 (61%)
Low Motivation	34 (83%)	9 (41%)	7 (39%)
Desire to Exercise Power			
High Motivation	14 (34%)	8 (36%)	9 (50%)
Low Motivation	27 (66%)	14 (64%)	9 (50%)

EXHIBIT 8
Initial Motivation to Manage and Level
of Subsequent Performance Rating
for Managers Who Separated

Motivation to Manage	Superior Would Not Rehire	Superior Would Rehire
High Motivation	12 (40%)	25 (81%)
Low Motivation	18 (60%)	6 (19%)
Favorable Attitude Toward Authority		
High Motivation	11 (37%)	18 (58%)
Low Motivation	19 (63%)	13 (42%)
Desire to Compete		
High Motivation	18 (60%)	23 (74%)
Low Motivation	12 (40%)	8 (26%)
Assertive Motivation		
High Motivation	14 (47%)	23 (74%)
Low Motivation	16 (53%)	8 (26%)
Desire to Exercise Power		
High Motivation	13 (43%)	23 (74%)
Low Motivation	14 (57%)	8 (26%)

The studies show that motivation to manage can *cause* success. The person who wants to compete, has a favorable attitude to authority, wants power, or wants to be in a distinctive position is the kind of person who is likely to get himself promoted into management and to move up fast once he gets there. These are the people who help themselves and their companies, too. They are the kind of managers that any profit-minded company should seek out and nurture. A great many nonbusiness organizations would benefit from their services as well.

Managers of this kind not only behave in ways that get them promoted, they behave in ways that produce high ratings on performance as well. In the Marketing and R & D Departments of the oil company there were a number of men who left the company during the time period covered by the study. The separation report form turned in to the Industrial Relations Department by the immediate superior of each departing manager contained an item asking whether rehiring was recommended if he should ever want to come back to the company. As we would expect, those who were recommended for rehire had a much higher level of initial motivation to manage than did those who were not recommended. A number of those with low managerial motivation who left the company were in fact fired.

An All-American Boy?

At this point the reader may be tempted to conclude that a person with strong motivation to manage will be good at anything he tries — that he sparkles with so much of the American ideal that he cannot be denied.

This does not appear to be the case. For instance, among dealer salesmen who handle relationships with retail service station owners for the oil companies, motivation to manage makes no difference at all in sales effectiveness. The records for gasoline, motor oil, and TBA (tires, batteries, and accessories) sales through stations handled by salesmen with high motivation to manage are no better than those for the territories of salesmen who lack this characteristic. Factors like a typically happy mood, a desire to be with people, and self-confidence do make a difference, but not motivation to manage.

The same is true of management consultants. No matter how one measures success — performance appraisals by superiors, compensation, per diem charges to clients for services — motivation to manage makes little difference. In this country (although not abroad), a strong desire for power does contribute to greater success as a consultant, but none of the other aspects of motivation to manage do. In a large public school district like Portland, motivation to manage is important; in smaller districts, where relationships are more informal, it has little, if any, relation to the performance ratings, position level, or pay of administrators. The professorial rank (assistant, associate, or full professor) achieved in a university is unrelated to managerial motivation.

In fact, there are even some jobs where motivation to manage can be a deterrent to success. The following results are from a group of physical scientists (not managers) in an industrial research lab:

	Unsuccessful	Successful
High Motivation to Manage	7 (64%)	3 (19%)
Low Motivation to Manage	4 (36%)	13 (81%)

Motivation to manage is a crucial ingredient of managerial effectiveness. There are other studies that I have not discussed — one that I conducted involving almost 500 managers in a large corporation, for instance; another carried out by Lynn Lacey at the China Lake, Cal., Naval Weapons Center, based on over 100 managers in the research laboratory there. All the studies point to the same conclusion. But motivation to manage is something that helps in managing, not in most other activites. Furthermore, on the basis of the research we have to date, I believe Marvin Bower is right when he says it is in companies with 300 or more employees that motivation to manage really makes a difference; below that size, it appears to be less important.

Motivation to manage is a major factor in what we call executive talent. Without it large organizations, whether public or private, may find themselves in serious managerial trouble. To the extent it becomes a scarce commodity, the American free enterprise system will operate less effectively; the system may even stumble and fall.

3

Motivation to Manage and Wanting To Be a Manager

A classic example of a situation illustrating the problems associated with deficient motivation to manage came to my attention several years ago when I was working on a consulting assignment. A young man, a scientist in his early thirties, had been hired by a large corporation from a small commercial research firm to head up a small but high-powered technical group composed primarily of physical scientists and economists. The company had been attracted by the man's considerable reputation for creative ideas and his ability to implement original approaches. Although the position was basically a managerial one, the company downplayed this aspect initially, offering as an inducement the opportunity to put into effect a variety of new kinds of programs, in addition to a substantial raise in salary.

It soon became apparent that the young man was totally lacking in motivation to manage. His approach was nondirective in the extreme. Decisions in the group, if they were made at all, emerged out of seemingly interminable meetings which took so much time that other work was severely disrupted. Paper work was delayed, phone calls went unreturned, and letters were not answered. A number of new approaches were introduced, but there was little followup, so that the programs often got badly off course before a problem was recognized. At one point the new manager took the initiative and actively divested himself of a major segment of his responsibilities, turning all authority for certain matters over to a subordinate. Furthermore, there were constant disagreements, and several episodes, best described as "blowups," with superiors.

In spite of this chaotic internal managerial situation, the young man continued to produce innovative ideas which attracted widespread attention in professional and industry circles. As a result he was approached by a number of firms regarding higher level managerial positions. At such times he was typically viewed as "playing hard to get" by the representatives of the companies that contacted him. He would ignore attempts to communicate, and the company representatives were thus forced to seek him out, at some inconvenience. As a result few offers actually were made, and those that were made were rejected.

Finally the company was forced to recognize its error in giving the young man major managerial responsibility. He was replaced as manager by another member of the group, who had in fact been actively "campaigning" for the position for some time, without any real opposition. The new manager was a former athletic coach who was very strongly motivated to manage.

The consistent pattern of avoidance exhibited by the young man is typical of those who lack motivation to manage—they avoid competition, avoid assertiveness, avoid the use of authority, avoid attracting attention, avoid basic responsibilities, and get on poorly with superiors. This pattern can be expected to result in poor managerial performance and a failure to move up. The lack of advancement may occur because the individual rejects an opportunity for promotion, or because he acts in such a way that it is not offered. However, it should also be possible to avoid managing by not going into managerial work in the first place.

An important way in which motivation *not* to manage may assert itself is in the choice of a career that does not involve managing—a profession, sales work, or an occupation based primarily on high technical skill or creativity. Actually, this is what the young man just discussed thought he was doing —furthering his professional career—when he went to work for the large company. He did not view the new position as essentially managerial, and the company initially encouraged him in this misperception.

This chapter considers the whole matter of career choice in the same way that Chapter 2 considers career success. If anything, career choice is even more important to a company. When low motivation to manage results in poor managerial performance, at least part of the job gets done. When low motivation to manage results in no one's being in the position at all, nothing gets done. The basic question under consideration is: Can a dearth of managerial motivation really mean that very few people will want to undertake careers in business management, with the result that many managerial jobs will go begging? Our studies indicate that it can.

Why College Students Want to Manage

I find that when I ask college students majoring in business administration what kind of future they are preparing for, what their goals are, and what they want to do in an occupational sense, several types of responses occur. There is a very small group, about 5 percent, who mention teaching; slightly over half indicate a specialized job within the business world, such as management consultant, market research analyst, advertising specialist, security analyst, life insurance underwriter, accountant, forester, training representative, labor relations specialist, systems engineer, insurance salesman, commercial loan specialist, and production engineer; and about 25 percent note managing, either in a specialized area or in the general management sense. The remainder either do not provide any specific answers, or mention one of a variety of nonbusiness occupations.

If motivation to manage makes a difference in the choice of a career, those who pick management should be predominantly the students with higher motivation to manage. This is in fact the case. And at the undergraduate level it is primarily a desire to compete, among the various aspects of managerial motivation, that guides the students to this choice of an occupation; those who enjoy competition are much more likely to have settled on a managerial career than those who do not, probably in response to the competitive nature of our free enterprise system.

In discussing careers with undergraduate students in their late teens and early twenties, one gets a strong feeling of uncertainty and indecision. Even those with intense desires of the kind that go to make up motivation to manage often do not

---

EXHIBIT 9
Motivation to Manage and the Career Choices
of Undergraduate Business Students

Motivation to Manage	Choosing a Business Specialty or Teaching	Choosing Business Management
High Motivation	32 (43%)	21 (64%)
Low Motivation	43 (57%)	12 (36%)

Desire to Compete		
High Motivation	37 (49%)	25 (76%)
Low Motivation	38 (51%)	8 (24%)

realize as yet that managerial work would provide them with what they want. They simply have not had the experience and exposure to know this, and most colleges lack the kind of trained vocational counseling services that could provide them with this information.

The connecting link between motivation to manage and a managerial career choice is not forged as frequently among undergraduate students as it should be. There is a major need for improved vocational guidance to remedy this situation, and in my opinion this guidance should be provided within the business schools themselves. One way to help alleviate future shortages of managerial talent would be to ensure that those young people who do possess motivation to manage have every opportunity to enter upon a managerial career.

The M.B.A. and D.B.A. Students

The undergraduate business students whose career choices and motives I have studied average twenty years of age. Graduate students working toward Master of Business Administration and Doctor of Business Administration degrees, on the other hand, tend to be considerably older. Many have had experience working for business firms. The average age of my M.B.A. students is twenty-five, and of the D.B.A. students twenty-nine. These people have had a much greater opportunity than the undergraduates to observe and in some cases to experience managerial work. Accordingly, those among them with strong motivation to manage should have learned that managing can offer them a satisfying career; those lacking motivation to manage should have settled on an alternative occupation.

At the graduate level, the proportion headed for teaching careers rises to something over 25 percent, largely due to the inclusion of D.B.A. students. The number choosing managing

also rises—to about one third. The business specialists constitute another 28 percent. The remaining group lacking a career
objective or, in a few cases, seeking a nonbusiness career, is
smaller than among the undergraduates—roughly 10 percent as
against 16 percent. Some kind of specific career choice is more
likely to have crystallized by the time one gets to graduate
school.

The graduate students with higher motivation to manage
are more likely to choose a career in business management, and
relatively few who lack motivation to manage indicate a managerial career choice. In this group the linking of motivation and
occupation has definitely occurred. In fact, every one of the various aspects of motivation to manage shows this relationship,
with one lone and very interesting exception. The students
headed for teaching careers are at least as likely to want to be in a
distinctive position at the center of attention as the managers;
those choosing a business specialty part company with the
teachers, as well as with the managers, with regard to this one
motive.

Actually, the finding that a desire to be in a distinctive position is strong among those starting on a career in teaching is not
surprising. The same might be expected of actors and actresses,
who also perform before large audiences. One of the reasons
that people are attracted to teaching appears to be that they like
to be in a unique position where a group of individuals focuses
attention on them, and the classroom or lecture hall situation
provides an ideal way to satisfy this desire.

Discussions with individual students indicate that a major
factor in the strong relationship between motivation to manage
and the choice of a managerial career at the graduate level is the
particular career strategy developed by a number of the students. Many say that they have come back to graduate school to
get an advanced degree in order to move up the managerial
ladder more rapidly. Faced with what appears to be at least a

EXHIBIT 10
Motivation to Manage and the Career Choices
of Graduate Business Students

Motivation to Manage	Choosing a Business Specialty	Choosing Teaching	Choosing Business Management
High Motivation	11 (33%)	11 (34%)	33 (80%)
Low Motivation	22 (67%)	21 (66%)	8 (20%)
Favorable Attitude Toward Authority			
High Motivation	8 (24%)	9 (28%)	21 (51%)
Low Motivation	25 (76%)	23 (72%)	20 (49%)
Desire to Compete			
High Motivation	13 (39%)	15 (47%)	30 (73%)
Low Motivation	20 (61%)	17 (53%)	11 (27%)
Assertive Motivation			
High Motivation	13 (39%)	8 (25%)	31 (76%)
Low Motivation	20 (61%)	24 (75%)	10 (24%)
Desire to Exercise Power			
High Motivation	15 (45%)	15 (47%)	32 (78%)
Low Motivation	18 (55%)	17 (53%)	9 (22%)
Desire for a Distinctive Position			
High Motivation	10 (30%)	23 (72%)	26 (63%)
Low Motivation	23 (70%)	9 (28%)	15 (37%)
Sense of Responsibility			
High Motivation	15 (45%)	10 (31%)	30 (73%)
Low Motivation	18 (55%)	22 (69%)	11 (27%)

temporary block to advancement in their present company, they gain admission to graduate school in the hope of either moving around the block or taking on a position in another company where they can become more thoroughly immersed in managing. In other words, those particular individuals in whom motivation to manage and the desire for a managerial career have become most closely interlocked are especially likely to go on to graduate work, as a means of achieving their goals. This, in my opinion, is a role that business education should play—that of making better and more successful managers of those who want to and can manage effectively.

Managers and University Professors Compared

One problem with the kind of analysis just described is that only career choices of students are considered. These preferences may change later, or those who want to move into managing may not actually do so. If one compares actual managers with teachers and business specialists, are the same kinds of motivational differences in evidence? Should this prove to be the case, we could have much more confidence in the view that those with little motivation to manage tend to prefer the business specialties and teaching over actual managing, and also, as a result, gravitate to these occupations. We could be a great deal surer that a lack of motivation to manage really does mean a lack of practicing managers.

My initial attempt to look into this question has been with university professors of business administration. These are individuals who by virtue of training and expertise have much of what is needed to become effective business managers. But they are not managers. Is it possible that the reason is a lack of motivation to manage?

Comparison of a group of university professors from several different business schools, all holding advanced degrees, with a similar group of business managers, also with advanced degrees, yields results not unlike those obtained with the graduate business students. High motivation to manage goes with being a manager; low motivation with university teaching. Even the tendency for teachers and managers to have an equally high desire for a distinctive position is repeated.

EXHIBIT 11
Motivation to Manage of Business Managers
With Advanced Degrees and University
Professors of Business Administration

Motivation to Manage	University Professors	Business Managers
High Motivation	17 (36%)	29 (64%)
Low Motivation	30 (64%)	16 (36%)
Desire to Compete		
High Motivation	14 (30%)	31 (69%)
Low Motivation	33 (70%)	14 (31%)
Assertive Motivation		
High Motivation	21 (45%)	32 (71%)
Low Motivation	26 (55%)	13 (29%)

Given two individuals who have proceeded after college to go into a graduate business school—one with high motivation to manage, and in particular a love of competition and a characteristic assertiveness; the other with few signs of motivation to manage of any kind, except perhaps some desire to be in a distinctive position—two very different career patterns can be expected. The first is more likely to end up a manager, the second a professor. There will be reversals of course, as a result of specific circumstances, but this is the probable outcome.

Management Consultants and Managers

The major alternative to a managerial career chosen by undergraduate business students with little motivation to manage, and a choice with much the same frequency as teaching among graduate students, is some type of business specialty. An example is management consulting. Do practicing management consultants, like professors, have lower motivation to manage than business managers?

To study this question, I chose a group of young consultants just starting on their careers with a general management consulting firm having as its clients many of the largest corporations in this country and overseas. I compared these young consultants with an equally young group of managers drawn from the types of companies the consulting firm serves.

A problem arises with this type of comparison, because by no means all of the young consultants are planning on a lifetime career in the consulting field. In counseling with them I find a number who view consulting work as a means to obtain broadening and diversified experience. Before long they hope to move on to vice presidencies in large corporations, or perhaps to the top spot in a smaller firm. The consulting experience is a way of bypassing the lower levels of management, much as graduate work is. But for these people the basic career choice remains managing. I would say that at least a third of the consultants fall in this category; in the final analysis they are really managers,

---

EXHIBIT 12
Motivation to Manage of Business Managers
and Management Consultants
(Business Specialists)

Motivation to Manage	Management Consultants	Business Managers
High Motivation	45 (48%)	37 (60%)
Low Motivation	48 (52%)	25 (40%)
Assertive Motivation		
High Motivation	38 (41%)	35 (57%)
Low Motivation	55 (59%)	27 (43%)
Desire to Exercise Power		
High Motivation	41 (44%)	39 (63%)
Low Motivation	52 (56%)	23 (37%)

not business specialists. Unfortunately, however, I have no way of identifying the particular individuals who are of this type within the specific group of management consultants studied.

Even with this handicap present, differences between the young consultants and the young managers do occur. In terms of overall motivation to manage, the handicap reduces these differences considerably, but on specific aspects of motivation to manage, in particular the desire for power and assertive motivation, the managers are definitely more likely to have the stronger motivation. This business specialty, like university teaching, attracts individuals with less motivation to manage than does the practice of management.

The studies with actual business specialists and managers yield the same results as the analyses of student career choices. It does appear that a shortage of motivation to manage can mean that fewer people are available to fill managerial positions.

Student Managers in a Simulated Company

At the risk of seeming repetitive, I would like to approach this problem of wanting to be a manager from a somewhat different direction, with a view to obtaining further confirmation of the point that managerial motivation makes a difference in the career a person ends up in. To do this, I will first describe a highly realistic simulation situation which permits studies of occupational choice and career patterns within a much more limited time span than in real life. By telescoping the time dimension, this simulation makes it possible to conduct analyses which would otherwise require years in a relatively short period of time.

This simulation, called Management Development Corporation (MDC), is the creation of the Management Department of Western Michigan University in Kalamazoo. MDC is operated by undergraduate students enrolled in management courses and exists only for training purposes. It provides an opportunity to learn at first hand what it is like to work in and to manage a company.

The students work on actual current problems. They provide services to the Management Department in the form of computer printouts, analyses of department studies, and data on class grades. They also undertake planning studies dealing with relevant activities, costs, scheduling of resources, etc. Information is developed for outside groups regarding Western Michigan University, its Management Department, and MDC; this includes brochures, newspaper articles, newsletters, and the like. Finally, the students work on personnel and administrative records related to MDC itself.

The company is headed by a president who reports to a three-man faculty board of directors. This board reviews and approves progress toward objectives, and receives final oral reports from management at the end of each semester. Performance appraisals are made by the students themselves. These appraisals, in the form of ratings by superiors, are subsequently converted into course grades.

Below the president are varying numbers of vice presidents, general managers, department managers, project managers, and, at the nonmanagerial level, a large group of staff analysts. Leadership is appointive, with promotion decisions made by student superiors. Promotion can occur at any time, but the largest changeovers occur at the beginning of each semester. Each top-management group selects its own successors. At a maximum, students stay in MDC for two years (usually as juniors and seniors), so that turnover in management positions is considerably accelerated over the real-life situation.

A high proportion of the nonmanagement staff analysts come from an introductory management course which is required of all business administration students. Students in this course do not have to enter MDC, however. They can complete the course in several different ways, although the grading pro-

EXHIBIT 13
Motivation to Manage and Being Chosen to
Manage in a Simulated Business Firm

Motivation to Manage	Not Chosen as Managers		Chosen as Managers
	Choosing Not to Join the Firm	Choosing to Join the Firm	
High Motivation	34 (44%)	125 (47%)	46 (63%)
Low Motivation	44 (56%)	139 (53%)	27 (37%)
Desire to Compete			
High Motivation	36 (46%)	143 (54%)	47 (64%)
Low Motivation	42 (54%)	121 (46%)	26 (36%)
Desire for a Distinctive Position			
High Motivation	27 (35%)	121 (46%)	37 (51%)
Low Motivation	51 (65%)	143 (54%)	36 (49%)
Sense of Responsibility			
High Motivation	34 (44%)	117 (44%)	50 (68%)
Low Motivation	44 (56%)	147 (56%)	23 (32%)

cedure does operate to provide an incentive to work in MDC.

Essentially, then, there are three types of students. There are those who do not choose to join MDC; these individuals are making a choice which precludes any possibility of becoming managers. There are, in addition, those who at the point in time in question either do not desire to or have not been selected to become managers in MDC; these are the staff analysts. Finally, there are those for whom personal and student-superior choices have combined to produce appointment to a managerial position. These individuals are in much the same situation as those appointed to management in a company, except that managerial tenure in MDC is typically much shorter.

The level of motivation to manage in these three groups

follows the pattern that would be predicted, based on the view that people with managerial motivation tend to gravitate to management and people without it move away. MDC managers are more competitive than the other two groups and they have a much greater sense of responsibility. They want to be in a distinctive position more than those who do not join MDC.

In the opinion of the management faculty at Western Michigan, this motivational pattern makes a great deal of sense. Those who enjoy competing strive to move up into management positions, and thus to win out. Those who are responsible and conscientious are selected for management positions because in a student-run organization such as MDC there is a particularly strong need for people who will in fact participate and do the work. Each group of managers, as it moves up to higher levels, needs help in getting its work done; accordingly, the group moving up taps those who exhibit motivation to do so to replace it in the lower management positions that are vacated. One of the major problems that the faculty has with MDC as a teaching device is that a number of students become only minimally involved and may do very little work.

As compared with other options, joining MDC requires more interaction with other students, more group work, and the possibility of making informal and formal presentations to other students and the faculty. Thus, those who prefer to work independently in the more traditional academic mode of reading, lectures, and exams are likely to choose not to join MDC because they do not want to take the risk of becoming the center of attention.

This analysis, using the time-telescoping simulation, leads to the same conclusion as do the studies of student career choices and of working adults. A lack of needed motivation to manage may not reduce the number of people who want to *work* in business firms, but it certainly can have an impact on the number who want and have the talent to *manage* them. This is where *the human constraint* becomes a reality. A firm cannot grow and develop if it does not have the managerial talent to do so.

4

Change on the Campus

In doing research it sometimes happens that the most important findings appear unexpectedly, as an outgrowth of a study undertaken for an entirely different purpose. This is the case with the findings reported in this chapter.

In early 1968, while working on one of the studies of student career choice discussed in Chapter 3, I was struck by the fact that the students, who happened to be from the University of Oregon, exhibited much lower motivation to manage than other students from the same University in 1960 and 1961. Since the University of Oregon had experienced considerable disruption in the interval, as a result of student demonstrations, it occurred to me that it might be of interest to look into managerial motivation levels at several other universities that had experienced outbreaks of student unrest, to see if there was any consistent relationship. Thus began a series of investigations into changes in motivation to manage on college campuses that has continued to the present time.

Overall Trends: 1960-73

In addition to the original group of University of Oregon students measured in 1960-61 and numbering 287, several of my graduate students and I have studied a number of college groups, as follows:

117 Portland State University students—1966-67
129 University of Oregon students—1967-68
122 University of Maryland students—1969
 48 Portland State University students—1970
349 Western Michigan University students—1971
 73 University of Maryland students—1972
 66 University of South Florida students—1972
 86 University of Oregon students—1972-73

The students all were in undergraduate business administration courses, and they are typical of such students at the particular university at the time noted. The basis for this conclusion is that motivation to manage was measured in courses required of all business majors, where a good cross section can be obtained, and not in courses with just accounting or marketing majors or the like. The courses generally are at the junior-year level, and the students' average age is in the early twenties. In all groups the great majority are males, with the number of females never exceeding 20 percent and usually approximating 10 percent. This is typical for business administration programs.

When the student groups are viewed in sequence over time, the results are striking. Motivation to manage has been dropping by something like 3 percent a year. Furthermore, there is no sign of an upswing in sight. Increasingly, it appears, the business schools are training people who do not have the motivation to manage and who are unlikely to do well at it if they try.

Because of the gap in our studies between 1961 and 1966, a period of sizable change, a question could be asked whether the data from the early 1960s might somehow be in error. This seems unlikely on several counts. First, there clearly has been a decline since 1966, so it would not be surprising that a similar

EXHIBIT 14
Motivation to Manage of Business
Administration Students: 1960-73*

Motivation to Manage	1960-61	1966-68	1969-70	1971	1972-73
High Motivation	184 (64%)	90 (37%)	69 (41%)	123 (35%)	68 (30%)
Low Motivation	103 (36%)	156 (63%)	101 (59%)	226 (65%)	157 (70%)
Favorable Attitude Toward Authority					
High Motivation	200 (70%)	123 (50%)	72 (42%)	150 (43%)	93 (41%)
Low Motivation	87 (30%)	123 (50%)	98 (58%)	199 (57%)	132 (59%)
Desire to Compete					
High Motivation	143 (50%)	75 (30%)	55 (32%)	105 (30%)	58 (26%)
Low Motivation	144 (50%)	171 (70%)	115 (68%)	244 (70%)	167 (74%)
Assertive Motivation					
High Motivation	197 (69%)	150 (61%)	90 (53%)	169 (48%)	99 (44%)
Low Motivation	90 (31%)	96 (39%)	80 (47%)	180 (52%)	126 (56%)
Desire to Exercise Power					
High Motivation	123 (43%)	113 (46%)	93 (55%)	183 (52%)	102 (45%)
Low Motivation	164 (57%)	133 (54%)	77 (45%)	166 (48%)	123 (55%)
Desire for a Distinctive Position					
High Motivation	136 (47%)	95 (39%)	74 (44%)	151 (43%)	109 (48%)
Low Motivation	151 (53%)	151 (61%)	96 (56%)	198 (57%)	116 (52%)
Sense of Responsibility					
High Motivation	151 (53%)	85 (35%)	55 (32%)	79 (23%)	69 (31%)
Low Motivation	136 (47%)	161 (65%)	115 (68%)	270 (77%)	156 (69%)

*Definitions of high and low motivation have been kept the same in Exhibits 14-17 to permit direct comparisons.

decline preceded 1966. Student activism first came clearly into the open at the University of California at Berkeley in 1964. If the decline in motivation to manage and the advent of campus upheavals are related (as I definitely believe they are), then the decline would date back at least to 1964, and probably earlier. Second, the 1960-61 group, with almost 300 students, is sufficiently large that the chances of error are minimized, and University of Oregon students studied in later years have differed little from those at other schools. Finally, another group of students, in education courses at the same school at the same time (1961), shows a similar level of managerial motivation. Of the business students, 64 percent are highly motivated; by the same definition, 70 percent of the 143 education majors are.

It seems probable that the shift in a negative direction on the campuses began in 1962 or 1963, primarily among the younger students. The impact appears to have been scattered at first, with many schools initially almost completely unaffected. We know, for instance, that the level of managerial motivation had not yet begun to decline at the University of Nevada in Reno in 1967, when the universities in Oregon already were heavily affected. At that time the University of Nevada had had no student unrest; the Oregon schools had.

It is my impression that the change came latest in the Rocky Mountain and Plains States, and in the South. By the early 1970s, however, it had permeated the entire country. Data from the University of South Florida in early 1972 are almost identical with what was found in other parts of the country at about the same time—and the University of South Florida began to experience the effects of student activism, including riots and arrests, in early 1972 also.

Motives That Changed and Motives That Did Not

One might anticipate that all aspects of the motivation to manage would change at once and to a similar degree, representing a comprehensive rejection of the managerial role in large organizations. This has not proved to be the case. Although the composite data available are plagued to some degree with the fluctuations that usually occur when the group used to represent one time period is drawn from a different place than the group representing another time period, it is still clear that some motives have declined and some have held stable, at least up to now. None has shown an overall increase.

Business students clearly are becoming more negative toward those in positions of authority. The shift in this aspect of motivation to manage is one of the most dramatic changes, and is entirely consistent with events on the campus—the attacks on public figures and the "establishment," the rebellion against university administrators, the hatred of law enforcement officers, and the emergence of the New Left with its continuing opposition to leaders of the free enterprise system. Many students have developed an antipathy to those who assume positions of authority which seems to have little relation to, and in fact often antedates, the actions for which those in authority are criticized.

A similar decline in competitive motivation is in evidence, especially in relation to occupational and career success. Large numbers of students simply do not care about "making it" any more, and take a dim view of the "the system," which emphasizes the values of hard work and economic striving. Cynicism regarding the competitive "rat race" is widespread. The noticeable attractiveness of the "hippy" life for young people is probably directly related to the decreasing desire to compete for the rewards that society has to offer.

The decrease in assertive motivation, although in evidence earlier, seems to be accelerating. The merging of masculine and feminine roles is clearly present in many sectors of society where the influence of young people can be felt—in the occupational sphere, in the home, in dress, in hair styles, and so on. On the college campus, and elsewhere too, young men appear to be increasingly rejecting those characteristics and behaviors which in the past have differentiated men from women. Homosexuality, if not more prevalent, has at least become more publicly acceptable among those of college age. These changes parallel the decline in measured assertive motivation to a striking degree.

Even with the decreases in other aspects of motivation to manage, however, there has been no overall change in the desire to exercise power over others. In fact, there appears to have been some increase in this type of motivation in the late 1960s and early 1970s, an increase which has by now evaporated. This pattern is entirely consistent with what has been happening on campus. Students have emphasized power-equalization and even student control. They have demanded the right to serve on university committees and to make decisions regarding student life, curriculums, university investments, and so forth. In the face of these demands, the traditional doctrine that the university administration stands *in loco parentis* has virtually disappeared. These and other considerations provide ample supporting evidence that college students have not shown any pervasive tendency to devalue or back away from the grasping of power.

The same lack of a decline is apparent with regard to the desire for a distinctive position, to be visible and the center of attention; there is no consistent trend of any kind. It is obvious that students have not shown any tendency to avoid visibility. They have taken over rostrums and lecterns to harangue audiences; they have urged each other on to riot; they have been anything but reticent in meetings of university bodies and at demonstrations. Observed behaviors are entirely consonant with the continuing prevalence of measured satisfaction in standing out and being the center of attention.

Finally, there is evidence of a decreasing sense of responsibility for routine matters. The day-to-day work that has to be done appears to have lost out to the appeal of the dramatic, to self-indulgence, and to hidden anxieties. Although newspaper and other accounts have made little of this point, those of us who have worked in universities through the years of turmoil have repeatedly found that many student activists find it difficult to suffer the demands of routine responsibility. They will fight tooth and nail to serve on a committee and then fail to show up when the committee meets. They cannot be relied upon to carry out the tasks of the university that they wish to control. The same lack of responsibility is in evidence in homework assignments, classroom preparation, and the current fad for paying others to carry out the drudgery of writing term papers. Again, the results of the studies and of general observation are so close that coincidence can hardly provide an explanation.

Individual Universities

Although comparisons of students at a single university in an earlier and later period have always identified a decline in overall motivation to manage, changes in individual motives have on occasion varied sharply from one school to another. At the University of Oregon, measurements at three points in time over a fourteen-year period reveal a pattern very close to that of the combined data; the aspects of motivation to manage that decrease are the same, although the magnitude of change appears to be somewhat greater. The overall measure shows a decrease at a rate of almost 3.5 percent per year at the University of Oregon, as compared with somewhat less that 3 percent for the combined data.

The University of Oregon findings are of particular interest, however, because they permit a determination of whether there has been any upswing, or return to normal, recently. If there has been, as some more optimistic reporters on the current scene have suggested, the change in the last five years should be considerably less than in the preceding seven years. On overall motivation to manage that is not the case; the drop is only from a 3.6-percent yearly rate to 3.2 percent. Furthermore, on some individual motives the decline has actually accelerated. This is true of both assertive motivation and desire to compete, and there has been no change whatsoever in the rate of decrease for favorable attitudes toward authority. The decline appears to be con-

EXHIBIT 15
Motivation to Manage of Business Administration
Students at the University of Oregon: 1960-73

Motivation to Manage	Years		
	1960-61	1967-68	1972-73
High Motivation	184 (64%)	50 (39%)	20 (23%)
Low Motivation	103 (36%)	79 (61%)	66 (77%)
Favorable Attitude Toward Authority			
High Motivation	200 (70%)	69 (53%)	35 (41%)
Low Motivation	87 (30%)	60 (47%)	51 (59%)
Desire to Compete			
High Motivation	143 (50%)	46 (36%)	19 (22%)
Low Motivation	144 (50%)	83 (64%)	67 (78%)
Assertive Motivation			
High Motivation	197 (69%)	80 (62%)	38 (44%)
Low Motivation	90 (31%)	49 (38%)	48 (56%)
Desire to Exercise Power			
High Motivation	123 (43%)	59 (46%)	36 (42%)
Low Motivation	164 (57%)	70 (54%)	50 (58%)
Desire for a Distinctive Position			
High Motivation	136 (47%)	56 (43%)	37 (43%)
Low Motivation	151 (53%)	73 (57%)	49 (57%)
Sense of Responsibility			
High Motivation	151 (53%)	48 (37%)	23 (27%)
Low Motivation	136 (47%)	81 (63%)	63 (73%)

tinuing unabated; not even a leveling off is in sight.

The picture at the University of Maryland differs much more markedly from the combined pattern than does that at Oregon. Maryland business students have declined in overall motivation to manage since 1969 at much the same rate as Oregon students and others, but not always on the same motives. This type of individual

variability from one school to another is to be expected; changes
that occur early at one location may not appear until several years

---

EXHIBIT 16
*Motivation to Manage of Business Administration
and Liberal Arts Students at the University
of Maryland: 1969-73*

Motivation to Manage	Business Administration		Liberal Arts
	1969	1972-73	1972-73
High Motivation	52 (43%)	27 (32%)	8 (13%)
Low Motivation	70 (57%)	58 (68%)	55 (87%)

Favorable Attitude Toward Authority			
High Motivation	59 (48%)	36 (42%)	28 (44%)
Low Motivation	63 (52%)	49 (58%)	35 (56%)

Desire to Compete			
High Motivation	40 (33%)	28 (33%)	13 (21%)
Low Motivation	82 (67%)	57 (67%)	50 (79%)

Assertive Motivation			
High Motivation	72 (59%)	30 (35%)	19 (30%)
Low Motivation	50 (41%)	55 (65%)	44 (70%)

Desire to Exercise Power			
High Motivation	72 (59%)	38 (45%)	14 (22%)
Low Motivation	50 (41%)	47 (55%)	49 (78%)

Desire for a Distinctive Position			
High Motivation	55 (45%)	47 (55%)	22 (35%)
Low Motivation	67 (55%)	38 (45%)	41 (65%)

Sense of Responsibility			
High Motivation	46 (38%)	33 (39%)	24 (38%)
Low Motivation	76 (62%)	52 (61%)	39 (62%)

later at another. In this context, the findings at the University of Maryland may signal the beginning of a more generalized decline in power motivation; it is too early yet to be sure. If this is the case, the result should be a considerable reduction in student pressure on university administrations for a major voice in university governance. There is, in fact, some evidence of this already.

Liberal Arts Students as Potential Managers

What has been said up to now is based on analyses of the motives of students in business administration courses. Most are business administration majors; a few are liberal arts majors, but only a few. When it has been possible to distinguish the liberal arts majors, they have proved to have even less managerial motivation than the business majors. However, their numbers are small, and liberal arts majors who take business courses cannot be assumed to be typical.

While it seems logical to assume that business administration students are more likely to provide a talent pool for business management than liberal arts majors, the latter are not entirely ruled out. A number of liberal arts students have gravitated to corporate management positions in the past, and no doubt this pattern will continue in the future. Given this situation, it is appropriate to ask whether students in the liberal arts might fill the gap created by the declining motivation to manage of business majors.

Studies conducted at the University of Maryland confirm the impressions gained from liberal arts majors in business courses: Liberal arts students, whether in physics, psychology, history, languages, or another discipline, have even less motivation to manage than business students. The data bearing on this point were gathered only recently, but from the fragmentary information available on liberal arts students registered in business courses in previous years, it seems likely that this has been true for some time. The managerial motivation of liberal arts students has probably been declining at much the same rate as, and thus parallel to, that of business students; they started lower and therefore they now show up as lower. This relative deficiency is most pronounced in overall motivation to manage, but it also appears to a significant degree in competitiveness, desire for power, and concern for a distinctive position. In any event, there is nothing to indicate that liberal arts students represent a vast talent pool to fill the void created by the decline in managerial motivation of business majors.

Furthermore, there is no reason to believe that the needed managerial talent can be located in other sectors of the university. Enough information is available on students in education, home economics, physical education, journalism, nursing, and the like to indicate that they are unlikely to exhibit more managerial motivation than business students; probably they will have less. In addition, the likelihood that these professional school students will find their way into business management positions is relatively remote.

Graduate Students in Business

Although the major focus of analysis has been on undergraduate students, data are available on graduate students in business administration as well; these are primarily students working toward a master's degree (M.B.A.) and preparing for a career in business.

In comparing such graduate students at the University of Oregon in 1964 with those of the 1972-73 period, we find a decline in overall motivation to manage that has occurred at a rate actually exceeding that for undergraduates at the same school—approximately 5 percent per year for the graduate students, as contrasted with somewhat less than 3.5 percent for the undergraduates. While the pattern of change among the various aspects of motivation to manage is similar to that for undergraduates, there are several discrepancies. For example, the current graduate students do not show the same degree of decline in competitiveness. They also appear to be less interested in being in a distinctive position, while no real decrease in this regard is in evidence among undergraduates.

EXHIBIT 17
Motivation to Manage of Graduate Business
Administration (M.B.A.) Students: 1964-73

Motivation to Manage	Years	
	1964	1972-73
High Motivation	29 (58%)	4 (15%)
Low Motivation	21 (42%)	22 (85%)
Favorable Attitude Toward Authority		
High Motivation	28 (56%)	5 (19%)
Low Motivation	22 (44%)	21 (81%)
Desire to Compete		
High Motivation	25 (50%)	9 (35%)
Low Motivation	25 (50%)	17 (65%)
Assertive Motivation		
High Motivation	38 (76%)	11 (42%)
Low Motivation	12 (24%)	15 (58%)
Desire to Exercise Power		
High Motivation	30 (60%)	15 (58%)
Low Motivation	20 (40%)	11 (42%)
Desire for a Distinctive Position		
High Motivation	32 (64%)	10 (38%)
Low Motivation	18 (36%)	16 (62%)
Sense of Responsibility		
High Motivation	23 (46%)	6 (23%)
Low Motivation	27 (54%)	20 (77%)

In the case of a desire to compete, at least, a ready explanation for the discrepancy is available. As noted in Chapter 3, many M.B.A. students seek the degree as a way of moving up fast and bypassing the competition. Some have been out in the business world and, finding their progress temporarily blocked, return to school in order to open up new opportunities. Others continue directly from their undergraduate studies in the hope of starting out at a higher level. Thus graduate business programs do tend to attract the more competitive students, the strivers. Competitive motivation has not suffered to the same degree as other aspects of motivation to manage among the graduate students because those who go on for the M.B.A. represent a special, more competitive group, rather than a cross section of college graduates.

Among the graduate students at the University of Oregon, the latest figures indicate that only 15 percent now have what would have been considered above-average motivation to manage in the early 1960s. This is not a unique finding. Among a group of master's-level students at the University of South Florida in 1972, the proportion with high motivation, similarly defined, was 20 percent. Actually, given the pervasiveness of motivational change at the undergraduate level, the finding of major declines of much the same nature at the graduate level is to be expected.

Managers and Students

In contrast with students, both undergraduate and graduate, analyses of the motivation to manage of practicing managers extending back to 1958 show little evidence of change. The motivational shift on campus has not as yet begun to impact on the corporate managerial hierarchy to any significant degree. This, of course, is to be expected. It has been scarcely ten years since the first signs of change appeared in the universities. These early students are now barely thirty. The decline in their managerial motivation was less pronounced than that of today's students, and few are yet of an age where movement into management positions would be expected. At best they have attained the lower rungs of the managerial ladder, where impact and visibility are least.

EXHIBIT 18

*Comparison of Early and Recent Business Students
and Business Managers for Motives
That Have Changed*

Motivation to Manage	1960-61 Students	1972-73 Students	1958-69 Managers
High Motivation	108 (38%)	21 (9%)	112 (47%)
Low Motivation	179 (62%)	204 (91%)	128 (53%)
Favorable Attitude Toward Authority			
High Motivation	121 (42%)	38 (17%)	117 (49%)
Low Motivation	166 (58%)	187 (83%)	123 (51%)
Desire to Compete			
High Motivation	143 (50%)	58 (26%)	132 (55%)
Low Motivation	144 (50%)	167 (74%)	108 (45%)
Assertive Motivation			
High Motivation	131 (46%)	52 (23%)	133 (55%)
Low Motivation	156 (54%)	173 (77%)	107 (45%)
Sense of Responsibility			
High Motivation	151 (53%)	69 (31%)	142 (59%)
Low Motivation	136 (47%)	156 (69%)	98 (41%)

Over the years since 1958 I have conducted studies of motivation to manage in a major oil company (at several points in time), in a large department store, in a wood-products firm, and in a baking company. The managers have varied in level from first-line supervisors to corporate officers. In every case the managers have averaged well above the students, and the disparity between the two groups is increasing, as the idea of a "generation gap" would suggest. Whereas differences between managers and students were relatively small around 1960, they are now of sizable magnitude. This is true of overall motivation to manage, and of attitudes toward authority, competitiveness, assertiveness, and sense of responsibility. While in the past manager-student differences in the proportion of people with high motivation were somewhat less than 10 percent, they are now three or four times that large.

Such fluctuations as have been observed among the managerial groups studied are small compared to the current manager-student differences, and appear to be attributable to the fact that certain functional areas attract managers with somewhat greater managerial motivation than other areas, just as the higher levels of management do. The greatest concentration of motivation to manage is in corporate sales and marketing departments. Managers in the accounting and financial areas, as well as in engineering and manufacturing, tend to be intermediate. R & D managers are relatively low, but still well above nonmanagers.

One would expect, from what has been said, that college students over thirty should look more like managers than younger students, and that managers under thirty should look more like students than older managers. In the first instance, at least, these expectations are borne out. A group of sixty-five business students at Portland State University, studied in 1970, contained approximately 25 percent who were thirty years of age or older. These older students had a distinctly higher level of motivation to manage, and in particular a much more favorable attitude to authority, than those in their twenties.

As to the expectation of finding low motivational levels among young managers, this also appears to be true. However, the business management groups studied recently have turned up only a handful of individuals under thirty; thus this kind of analysis does not provide as much information as could be desired. Much more convincing is a study of young junior professionals and management trainees hired directly from college by a large government research center. A comparison of those hired in successive years since 1967 indicates a definite decline in managerial motivation over time. This study is being conducted by psychologists at the research center, and represents an independent confirmation of my own findings.

Managers in Business and Government

In our society there is a widespread belief, expecially in the business sector, that business managers are generally more effective than managers in government. This impression is attributed to a variety of factors, including the greater rewards available in business, the greater independence of action, the freedom from political involvements, and the facilitating effects of a competitive economic system. It is assumed that these factors combine to make managing in large corporations more attractive to the country's outstanding managerial talent, and that federal, state, and local governments often attract individuals of somewhat lesser managerial capabilities.

My own studies of managerial motivation in government, although limited in scope, tend to support these beliefs. Furthermore, when combined with the data on motivational changes on campus, they indicate that in years to come the business sector will be lucky if it attracts even that level of managerial talent that now is found in government.

Most of the government managers I have studied worked as administrators in four school districts, and ranged in level from vice principals to superintendents. A separate study of twenty-five managers in a state employment service produced comparable results, however.

EXHIBIT 19
Motivation to Manage of Managers in
Business and Government

Motivation to Manage	Business	Government
High Motivation	164 (68%)	83 (34%)
Low Motivation	76 (32%)	161 (66%)

Favorable Attitude Toward Authority		
High Motivation	117 (49%)	128 (52%)
Low Motivation	123 (51%)	116 (48%)

Desire to Compete		
High Motivation	132 (55%)	101 (41%)
Low Motivation	108 (45%)	143 (59%)

Assertive Motivation		
High Motivation	133 (55%)	86 (35%)
Low Motivation	107 (45%)	158 (65%)

Desire to Exercise Power		
High Motivation	135 (56%)	69 (28%)
Low Motivation	105 (44%)	175 (72%)

Desire for a Distinctive Position		
High Motivation	147 (61%)	122 (50%)
Low Motivation	93 (39%)	122 (50%)

Sense of Responsibility		
High Motivation	142 (59%)	92 (38%)
Low Motivation	98 (41%)	152 (62%)

The government managers typically have less overall motivation to manage than business managers, and this difference is reflected in most of the specific aspects as well. That it does not emerge very markedly in the comparisons involving a desire for a distinctive position is not surprising, since the school administrators were almost invariably teachers first, and teachers tend to be strongly motivated along these lines. The state employment service managers have much less of this type of motiva-

---

EXHIBIT 20
Motivation to Manage of Graduate Students
Preparing for Managerial Careers in
Business and Government
(1964-66)

Motivation to Manage	Business	Government
High Motivation	29 (71%)	18 (32%)
Low Motivation	12 (29%)	39 (68%)

Favorable Attitude Toward Authority		
High Motivation	21 (51%)	22 (39%)
Low Motivation	20 (49%)	35 (61%)

Desire to Compete		
High Motivation	30 (73%)	23 (40%)
Low Motivation	11 (27%)	34 (60%)

Assertive Motivation		
High Motivation	31 (76%)	24 (42%)
Low Motivation	10 (24%)	33 (58%)

Desire to Exercise Power		
High Motivation	32 (78%)	22 (39%)
Low Motivation	9 (22%)	35 (61%)

Desire for a Distinctive Position		
High Motivation	26 (63%)	37 (65%)
Low Motivation	15 (37%)	20 (35%)

Sense of Responsibility		
High Motivation	30 (73%)	26 (46%)
Low Motivation	11 (27%)	31 (54%)

tion, and in this regard are probably more typical of government managers. The one area where government and business managers do not differ is in their attitudes toward authority; the attitudes of both are equally favorable, and are clearly distinguishable from those of students in recent years.

The conclusions drawn from comparisons of practicing business and government managers are backed up by analyses of the managerial motivation of University of Oregon graduate students who were preparing for jobs in business management and public school administration in the 1964-66 period. Again, the business group exhibits much stronger motivation. Again there is no meaningful difference in the desire to be in a distinctive position. Differences in attitudes toward authority are again small relative to other aspects of managerial motivation.

The Managerial Talent Shortage

As I review the findings discussed in these first four chapters, I can only conclude that the country is faced with a massive managerial talent shortage which can be expected to become progressively worse as the cohort caught up in these motivational changes advances in age, and current managers move on into retirement and die. Even if the present trends were to begin reversing themselves tomorrow, the country would be faced with a fifteen-year deficit in managerial talent, thus putting the free enterprise system to the greatest test it has faced since the Depression of the 1930s at least. For reasons to be discussed at length in the next two chapters, I believe such a spontaneous reversal is highly unlikely.

One could argue, of course, that students will be forced into managerial jobs by a need for money, in spite of their lack of managerial motivation. Once there they might be expected to change as a result of exposure to managerial work, so that ultimately their will to manage would rise to the levels currently in evidence among practicing managers. This suggestion is appealing. It has something of a "boys will be boys" quality, and reflects the old view that a fling at socialism and leftist involvement among the young need not be taken too seriously, because the realities and responsibilities of later life ultimately will prove sobering and provide the necessary corrective influence.

The problem is that at the present time we have a phenomenon which has not occurred in isolated individuals, but which pervades, characterizes, and is perpetuated by a massive "youth culture." We know that this phenomenon extends from college into graduate school, and on into the employment context. Now companies are reporting that they have increasing difficulty in getting their younger managers to accept promotions involving transfers to new locations, and that social concerns often appear to be of greater importance to young managers than either company profits or individual success.

None of this proves that these young managers will not change later on, and become increasingly motivated to manage, perform effectively, and contribute to corporate goals, much as more experienced managers do now. But if that happens merely as a consequence of serving in a managerial position for a period of time, with no deliberate effort to induce motivational change, it will certainly represent something very new on the corporate scene. The research has never provided any evidence that motivation to manage is likely to change unless something is done to make it change.

I have remeasured business school students over periods as long as two years, and managers over three- to four-month periods, with no sign of increased motivation. More convincing, however, is the repeated finding that individuals in their fifties and sixties with many years experience in managerial work have no greater motivation to manage than younger managers in their thirties and forties. Without some kind of specific intervention aimed at producing motivational change, such change does not appear to occur. Given what is now known, I would be much more willing to bet that increasing numbers of young managers will either drop out of the corporate "rat race" or continue as relatively ineffective managers than that a spontaneous generation of the will to manage will eventually occur.

Some idea of the magnitude of the problem ahead can be gleaned by comparing the measured level of managerial motivation among current students with that of business managers. In the 1972-73 period, information has been obtained on a total of 376 students, including business, nonbusiness, undergraduate, and graduate students. Only thirty of these students, less than 8 percent, have a motivation to manage which rises to the level of that of the *average* business manager whose motivation has been measured.

5

Change in Broad Perspective

It is obvious that the changes in motivation to manage described in Chapter 4 have not occurred in isolation. There is no question that there also have been changes in such areas as student activism, drug use, dress, and sexual behavior. In addition, there has been a great deal of speculation regarding changes in values, attitudes, and motives. Unfortunately, however, much of the writing and discussion in this area turns out to be just that — speculation. What is needed are good, solid measures of values, attitudes, and motives taken at various points in time, so that we can be sure whether or not change really has occurred.

Although data of this kind are limited, they do exist. Furthermore, they provide a valuable perspective within which changes in managerial motivation and the predicted executive talent shortage may be viewed.

Julian Rotter's Research on Trust and Control

Professor Julian Rotter, of the University of Connecticut, has been administering a scale designed to measure degree of trust in others to students at the university since 1964. Each year there has been a sizable drop in scores compared to those for the preceding year. A similar finding has been obtained with a somewhat different measure of trust among students at Peabody University, in a study extending back to 1954. Thus, the decline does not appear to be specific to either one measurement process or one university.

The tendency for students to be increasingly distrusting is most pronounced with regard to people in positions of authority in our society and in our organizations. There has been relatively little change with regard to people with whom the students have direct contact — parents, repairmen, salesmen — ordinary people. Of his findings Professor Rotter says, "The decline in trust . . . appears . . . to indeed be precipitous, and should it continue, our society would be in serious trouble, if it is not so already."

A second, and related, research program has been undertaken by Professor Rotter in the area of perceived sources of control. Here he has been concerned with the tendency of people either to feel they can control their own destiny through their own efforts, or to feel that they are controlled by forces in their environments, by fate, and by other people. Those who attribute control to themselves expect to be able to influence others, rate high on achievement, and view themselves as self-confident; they would seem to be the kinds of people who would espouse the Protestant work ethic and would do well in the context of a free enterprise system.

Yet Professor Rotter's research indicates that it is the sense of being powerless and at the mercy of one's environment that is on the increase. In tandem with the decline in trust there has been a decline in the feeling of being personally able to influence the distrusted external world — a decline not in the desire for power, but in the expectation of being able to exercise it. The studies go back to 1962 and indicate a similar pattern across the country, although the Midwest campuses appear to have been affected somewhat less than those on either coast. Professor

Rotter comments, "Our society . . . desperately needs as many active, participating internal-minded members as possible. If feelings of external control, alienation, and powerlessness continue to grow, we may be headed for a society of dropouts — each person sitting back, watching the world go by."

Studies on Authoritarianism

The subject of authoritarianism has been a source of much controversy in the social sciences. Some view the trait as reflecting Fascist tendencies, prejudice, and inflexibility — and there are research data to support this view. Others see it as reflecting leadership, commitment to hard work, and rationality — and there are research data to support this conclusion, too. In any event, it does seem clear that the authoritarian person is likely to be respectful of higher authority and to be willing to take orders from those of superior status. He has a strong sense of the legitimacy of authority, both of others and his own. He is thus drawn to and comfortable in organizations with the typical pyramid of managerial authority, and tends to reject more participative or democratic leadership styles, at least in the context of his own work situation and everyday life. The matter of authoritarianism is important both because changes in this regard among college students have been widely hypothesized and because some relationship to managerial motivation might be expected. Both turn out to be true.

Professor Daniel Ondrack, at the University of Toronto, has made an extensive compilation of studies conducted since the middle 1950s on the authoritarianism of college students. He finds a regular decline in scores over time. Professors Mervin Freedman, of San Francisco State College, and Paul Kanzer, of the University of Massachusetts, report a similar decline, based on studies conducted on various campuses, also since the middle 1950s. Their scales measure not only authoritarianism, but also what they call rebellious independence and impulse expression. The sharp decline in authoritarianism is matched by a similar rise in rebelliousness and uncontrolled expression of emotional impulses.

The parallel decline in motivation to manage and in authoritarianism reflects the presence of a relationship between

EXHIBIT 21

Motivation to Manage and Authoritarianism
Among College Students

Motivation to Manage	Level of Authoritarianism		
	Low	Medium	High
High Motivation	12 (32%)	19 (51%)	23 (64%)
Low Motivation	25 (68%)	18 (49%)	13 (36%)
Favorable Attitude Toward Authority			
High Motivation	15 (41%)	19 (51%)	23 (64%)
Low Motivation	22 (59%)	18 (49%)	13 (36%)
Desire to Compete			
High Motivation	15 (41%)	19 (51%)	21 (58%)
Low Motivation	22 (59%)	18 (49%)	15 (42%)
Assertive Motivation			
High Motivation	18 (49%)	22 (59%)	23 (64%)
Low Motivation	19 (51%)	15 (41%)	13 (36%)
Desire to Exercise Power			
High Motivation	18 (49%)	22 (59%)	23 (64%)
Low Motivation	19 (51%)	15 (41%)	13 (36%)
Desire for a Distinctive Position			
High Motivation	12 (32%)	13 (35%)	18 (50%)
Low Motivation	25 (68%)	24 (65%)	18 (50%)
Sense of Responsibility			
High Motivation	10 (27%)	18 (49%)	18 (50%)
Low Motivation	27 (73%)	19 (51%)	18 (50%)

the two. The relationship is certainly not great enough to justify interpreting motivation to manage as synonymous with authoritarianism; there is a great deal more to it than that. But the relationship is of sufficient magnitude to be considered meaningful.

Among the various aspects of managerial motivation, one stands out as being particularly related to authoritarianism. Not unexpectedly, this is a favorable attitude toward authority. It is true that this is the aspect of motivation to manage that one would expect to find related to authoritarianism, yet none of the aspects is entirely unrelated. Basically, the person who has the will to manage tends to be somewhat authoritarian. It is worth noting that this finding emerges from a study of a cross section of college students at the University of Maryland, an appropriate research context since the declines in motivation to manage and authoritarianism also were established in studies of college students.

Changes in Values

There have been a number of studies based on measures of human values — conceptions of good and bad, right and wrong, desirable and undesirable — which reveal the dimensions of the change on college campuses. These studies serve to expand on the scope of the change which has occurred, and they also indicate the particular and continuing importance of authority relationships.

Professors Lehman and Hill conducted surveys of the values of incoming freshmen at Michigan State University throughout the 1960s. Among other things, they note a decreasing concern about the future and a shift to moral values relative to the situation and group involved, thus indicating a decline in adherence to moral absolutes. An increasing degree of questioning of university authority also was in evidence.

A more extensive and lengthy inquiry was carried out by

Professors Charles Morris and Linwood Small, of the University of Florida, at a wide range of different colleges. Students were surveyed in 1970 and the results compared with those obtained using the same measure in the early 1950s. The more recent students place less value on social restraint, self-control, and progress through action and more on withdrawal, self-sufficiency, social concern, and self-indulgence. The data indicate that these values are particularly characteristic of the roughly 50 percent of students who feel that society as it exists today does not permit them sufficient opportunity to develop their abilities and express their wishes. This appears to be the same sense of powerlessness and being at the mercy of external forces described by Professor Rotter.

Some recent work done by Professor Ondrack with students at the University of Toronto and at the University of Michigan emphasizes the increasing desire for independence that others have noted. His studies also point to a greater desire for relationships within one's own age and peer group as contrasted with status and authority relationships, and an increased social concern. In general, Professor Ondrack concludes that the college students have shifted their values away from those characteristic of business executives and in the direction of those of university professors — from those of managers to those of professionals.

The Harvard Business School Research

As part of a comprehensive study of student expectations of corporate life, Professors Lewis Ward and Anthony Athos, of Harvard, administered a questionnaire measuring an individual's perception of himself to students in 1962 and in 1970. The 1962 students came from thirty-three different universities, and all were headed for positions in business. Within this group, the Harvard Business School students proved to be very little different from those in other universities in the characteristics measured. For this reason, and to save effort and expense, the 1970 students were all drawn from the Harvard Business School. The measure used requires the students to choose among pairs of adjectives (some pairs favorable and some pairs unfavorable) so as to provide descriptions of themselves.

The changes noted over the eight-year period seem to point up certain themes often heard on campuses today, as well as many of the findings from studies already discussed. In Profes-

---

EXHIBIT 22
Student Self-Perceptions in 1970
as Compared to 1962

Favorable Adjectives

More Preference For	Less Preference for
jolly	respectable
kind	popular
resourceful	foresighted
civilized	dignified
assured	careful
practical	industrious
sympathetic	patient
attractive	cautious
sharp-witted	deliberate
enterprising	intelligent

Unfavorable Adjectives

More Preference For	Less Preference For
impatient	day dreamer
loud	forgetful
egotistical	apathetic
outspoken	dissatisfied
intolerant	meek
cocky	tightfisted
cynical	militant

As reported by Lewis Ward and Anthony Athos in *Student Expectations of Corporate Life: Implications for Management Recruiting,* published by Harvard Business School in 1972.

sors Ward and Athos' terms these are, *"love* (self and other), *down with the establishment* (less emphasis on respectability and dignified style), *power to the people* (don't just passively accept or withdraw), *let go* (don't hold back in fear), *do it* (don't just be dissatisfied), *get in the action* (operate, don't administrate)."

The study tends to confirm the change to greater social concern, more negative attitudes toward established authority, and more uncontrolled emotional expression that others have noted, and it does so among students at a business school which has won worldwide renown as a source of top-level executive talent. The implications for future corporate management staffing require little elaboration at this point. However, I will return to other aspects of this study later in this chapter.

What They Think

Although studies which contrast motives, values, and attitudes at one point in time with those in evidence later on are most helpful in identifying changes that have occurred parallel to the changes in motivation to manage, the findings from these longitudinal analyses can be elaborated using studies of current attitudes. Two of the most interesting of these attitude surveys were conducted for *Fortune* and *Psychology Today* at the end of the 1960s.

The *Fortune* survey, conducted by Daniel Yankelovich, covered a variety of topics and included respondents of college age who had not continued their education, as well as those who had. It is of greatest interest, however, for the insights it provides into the attitudes toward authority of the college students sampled. In order to study the generation gap, the students were asked to indicate whether certain attitudes were more typical of them or their parents. In terms of those factors which most sharply differentiate the two groups, the parents are depicted as more compromising, more respectful of authority, less tolerant, less interested in people, less principled, less open, less interested in beauty, and less self-centered. In general the students are quite critical of their parents, especially when their responses are viewed in terms of what is known about their own values. The students view themselves as particularly tolerant and open and strikingly devoid of respect for authority. One suspects that when the students say they are tolerant they are thinking of their attitudes toward peers and age-mates, rather than their attitudes toward parents and those in positions of authority.

Furthermore, the students indicate a considerable unwillingness to accept the restraints of authority, whether reflected in society's laws or in the form of constraint by an employing organization. Close to one half find it difficult to accept the power and authority of a boss at work. Draft resistance and civil disobedience are as likely to be considered justified as they are to be rejected.

The *Psychology Today* survey, conducted by Jeffrey Hadden, occurred at roughly the same time, in 1969, and also involved many students from many campuses. The questions, however, were somewhat different in form and content than those used in the *Fortune* survey. As a result, the antiauthority theme is somewhat less in evidence and the independence and freedom-of-expression themes are more pronounced. Yet the overall conclusion is the same: "Their predominant mood is the rejection of authority and the desire to follow their own modes of conduct." To the question of whether universities should try to control student life outside the classroom, 79 percent answer in the negative. And 82 percent feel that they would not sacrifice their private lives, even if this should mean making less money.

A more recent *Fortune* analysis, by Edmund Faltermayer, published in March 1973, bears the headline, *Protest is gone, but its legacies have influenced an entire generation. Today's young are irreverent, yet full of a new tolerance and other surprises.* The implica-

EXHIBIT 23
Attitudes Expressed by College Students

Perceptions of . . .	self . . . as opposed to . . . parents	
Likely to compromise with things not liked	18%	50%
Respectful of those in authority	6%	48%
Tolerant of the views of others	58%	18%
Interested in people	46%	14%
Tendency to act based on beliefs	42%	11%
Openness to the world outside	59%	8%
Interested in beauty	42%	9%
Self-centered	49%	12%

Percent *unwilling* to accept restraints of law and authority:	
Abiding by laws not agreed with	71%
Restrictions on decisionmaking power when first employed	68%
Conformity pressures in dress and grooming	62%
Authority of a boss in the work situation	43%
Extent of support for draft resistance	49%
Extent of support for civil disobedience	46%

Adapted from a survey reported in the January 1969 issue of *Fortune*.

tion, based on a much less comprehensive and systematic survey than the one done in 1969, is that certain reversals have occurred since then, with the major focus on a new tolerance. Yet tolerance was strongly in evidence before, and the tolerance described in 1973 is clearly the same as that described in 1969 — a tolerance for behavior on the part of peers that those who are older might well condemn. That protest behavior has decreased does not mean that motives and attitudes have changed. They may merely be directed toward new types of behavior. None of the data currently available, including the 1973 data on motivation to manage and the *Fortune* data on tolerance, provide a basis for concluding that reversals of the trends discussed in this and the preceding chapter have yet come about.

Attitudes Toward Business and Managing

Attitudes of college students toward business careers are of particular importance in a consideration of the supply of managerial manpower because they often condition early occupational choices. A number of surveys have dealt with this subject, including the 1969 *Fortune* survey. There the picture which emerged was ambiguous. Business was viewed by the majority of student repondents as competitive, making a major contribution, a key element for the future, and a major factor in society; but also as requiring conformity, being large and overwhelming, not having very high ethics, and not allowing for individuality. Roughly one third of the college students made it clear that they definitely did not want to become involved in business, and only one quarter gave a business career a solid yes vote. Data presented by Thomas Benham, president of Opinion Research Corporation, based on that organization's surveys over the years, make it clear that these attitudes toward business reflect a distinct negative shift since the early 1950s.

There is good reason to believe that the college experience itself typically has a negative impact on attitudes toward business. Studies conducted by Leslie Dawson at Michigan State University reveal that the attitudes of students in their junior and senior years are much more unfavorable than those of freshmen and sophomores. This negative shift is most pronounced in the liberal arts group; it does not occur among business administration students.

A recent study conducted by Rosalind Barnett and Professor Renato Tagiuri, of the Harvard Business School, utilized data obtained through the readers of the *Harvard Business Review* from over 2,500 young people ranging in age from nine to seventeen. A high proportion had managers as parents, and the group as a whole proved to be unexpectedly well informed about managerial work. Yet interest in a managerial career was far from overwhelming. When asked what they would most like to do when they grew up, 40 percent of the males and 20 percent of the females mentioned either management or business. But 50 percent of both the males and the females indicated that management was what they would *least* like to go into. Clearly there are a great many children, even in families that would be expected to produce the managers of the future, who do not want to manage.

Much the same conclusion emerges from a study conducted by Professors Daniel Braunstein and George Haines, of the University of Rochester, among 4,000 high school students. The career of business executive was about intermediate in preference among those studied, with a value of -1 on a scale from +100 to -100. However, it was clearly viewed less favorably than that of research scientist or of lawyer. Furthermore, this scale value drops to -7 among the students who intend to go on to college — the most crucial group. It is -15 among the girls.

Business organizations also rate as intermediate as a place of employment, being less desired than the Federal Government or a college faculty. However, the large corporations are viewed more favorably than small businesses, and their scale value of +5 places them well above an executive career in rated preference. Professors Braunstein and Haines comment, "There may be a significant difference between a career as a business executive and a career in a business organization. Apparently many students would find work in a business organization satisfying if it involved a nonbusiness career such as law or research." The implication appears to be that managing in business is viewed more negatively than holding a number of other nonmanagerial jobs in the same context.

These and other studies seem to add up to the conclusion that negative sentiments toward business careers are on the increase, and that it is managing in particular that is being rejected. A study by Professors Donald DeSalvia and Gary Gemmill, of Syracuse University, indicates as one of the major problems that students grossly misperceive the values of current managers. They see managers as being more "organization men" than they really are. Yet a considerable residue of positive sentiment remains, and even the managerial job is rated positively in terms of advancement opportunity and salary.

EXHIBIT 24
Preference (On a Scale from +100 to -100)
for Various Careers and Organizations
Among High School Students.

Careers

Research Scientist	+11
Lawyer	+11
Business Executive	−1
College Professor	−8
Counseling Psychologist	−16

Organizations

Federal Government	+14
College Faculty	+14
Large Corporation	+5
Small Business	−4
Nonprofit Service Organization	−29

Adapted from an article by Daniel Braunstein and George Haines in the February 1971 issue of *Business Horizons*.

What Do They Want?

From some research that has been done with regard to motivation to manage by Benjamin Gantz, Clara Erickson, and Robert Stephenson, under the auspices of the Center for Creative Leadership, it is possible to infer which occupations are likely to be increasingly rejected and which ones increasingly preferred. As motivation to manage declines in the college-age population, we can expect to find fewer graduates with interests similar to those of people in such occupations as army officer, personnel director, vocational counselor, credit manager, sales manager, and YMCA physical director — people who tell others what to do, primarily in the context of large organizations. On the other hand, the number of graduates with the interests of artists, architects, dentists, mathematicians, chemists, and journalists — all professionals or semiprofessionals — can be expected to increase.

There is considerable evidence that college students, especially those with better grades, are now looking in their careers for such things as interesting work, opportunity for advancement, opportunity for self-development, and freedom on the job. These expressed desires are entirely consistent with what is known about their motives and values. It appears that these desires are seen as more likely to be achieved in the professions than in managing.

The Harvard Business School research provides further insight into the kind of company that students want to work in. Information on this point was obtained in both 1962 and 1970 and, as might be expected, there have been some drastic changes. The most pronounced increases have been in the number of students who prefer small companies and in the wish to have the company actively involved in community needs (social concern).

On the other hand, there are a number of company characteristics for which the student preferences show decreases. The students appear to have shifted sharply in the direction of wanting more from the company and giving it less. They are no longer willing to forego fringe benefits, and they want a top man-

---

EXHIBIT 25
Differences Between 1962 and 1970 Students
in Characteristics of Preferred Companies

	1962	1970
Preferred more in 1970		
a small company	45%	74%
a company trying to meet community needs	60%	84%
Preferred less in 1970		
a company having few fringe benefits	52%	20%
a company where they would have to prepare many reports	48%	23%
a company requiring membership in professsional organizations	45%	23%
a company requiring membership in business organizations	44%	22%
a company where punctuality is important	53%	31%
a company where pleasing superiors results in promotion	62%	42%
a company where top management's major concern is profits	74%	56%
a company where prestige is based on education	40%	22%
a company exerting continual pressure to reduce costs	65%	50%
a company where top management pays close attention to operations	79%	64%
a company where a pleasing personality helps one to get ahead	77%	62%

As reported by Lewis Ward and Anthony Athos in *Student Expectations of Corporate Life: Implications for Management Recruiting,* published by Harvard Business School in 1972.

---

agement that is not too concerned with profits, costs, and the like—presumably a top management that will share with them their concern for social action. They do not want to do routine administrative work, such as writing reports, and there is a strong desire to get away from restraints, rules, and pressures that might limit their freedom. Finally, they do not want to have to be nice to anyone in order to get ahead. Again and again the students of today are saying that they want the company to give them more of what they want (freedom, social action, advancement) but in return are willing to give less in terms of effort, loyalty, and permitted discretion to the company to regulate their behavior.

In commenting on these patterns, Professors Ward and Athos sound a somber note that in many respects echoes my own concerns. They ask, "Unless the great corporations can attract and keep their share of talented young men, can it be that the ultimate limitation on the concentration and effectiveness of corporate power and service may not be legal constraint but rather the slow starvation of large corporations for lack of future managerial talent? . . . We think the question is not too dramatic to pose seriously." This sums up about as well as anyone can what I mean by *the human constraint.*

Professors Ward and Athos report that their students are, in fact, flocking to the smaller companies, and we know that a major reason students reject the larger corporations is that they consider them a poor place to achieve their values. College students exhibit a strong preference for companies perceived as reflecting attitudes and values much like their own, and reject those which they view as having dissimilar images. Since many of the larger firms clearly project images antithetical to the attitudes and values of increasing numbers of college students, many of these companies can be expected to face major difficulties in attracting managerial talent in the future. Yet there is a serious question as to how far large business organizations can move in the direction of student values and still survive.

Company Experience

Less systematic study has been made of the younger generation in actual company contexts than has been made on college campuses, primarily because it is easier to obtain data from college students. In general, however, it appears that the attitudes, values, and motives identified on campus are carried into the business world unmuted, and in many cases they have created severe problems for employing organizations.

A recent American Management Association survey, conducted by Dale Tarnowieski, indicates considerable dissatisfaction among younger managers. In particular there is concern about opportunities for personal growth and development, and about the arbitrariness of promotion decisions by superiors. A *Fortune* study, conducted by Judson Gooding, repeatedly notes the same characteristics among managers under thirty that have been identified among college students. A 1971 survey of the members of the American Society for Personnel Administration, conducted by Prentice-Hall, indicates marked concern among personnel managers over the problem of adapting company practices to the demands of the younger generation. Many of the same problems were evidenced in a similar survey conducted by The Bureau of National Affairs, Inc., toward the end of 1969.

Companies apparently experienced very little of this effect until late 1969 or 1970. One personnel executive, who has been involved in recruiting and selecting management trainees from among the M.B.A. graduates of the major business schools for many years, notes a drastic change at about this time. Social concerns began to come to the forefront, and many candidates gave them more emphasis than either the economic success of the company or their own personal success. This shift in attitudes and motives manifested itself in a number of different selection procedures.

One company has noted a marked increase in refusals of geographic transfers among younger managers. Another has practically had to discontinue the practice of having senior executives conduct informal discussions with new management trainees because of the tensions generated. Reports of refusals of job offers and requests for transfers because of ethical concerns over the marketing of particular products are increasing. This is anecdotal evidence, but there are a great many such anecdotes around in the business world today.

It might seem, with this kind of situation existing in companies, that a feedback effect would combine with existing campus attitudes to severely limit enrollment in the country's business schools. My own belief is that this will not occur to any significant extent, because business schools train students for a great many occupations other than that of corporate manager, and many are making a concerted effort to bring this fact to the attention of the public.

The survey conducted by Professors Braunstein and Haines indicated that nonmanagerial jobs in business, especially professional positions, are viewed more positively than managing. Professors Ward and Athos note the appeal of small companies. An increasing number of business school graduates are bringing their skills to nonbusiness organizations. To the extent the business schools train teachers, entrepreneurs, consultants, accountants, financial analysts, market researchers, and the like, there should be relatively little effect on the total demand for their services. However, a continuing change in the mix of students can be anticipated, with the number headed for corporate management declining significantly.

Dimensions of Change

As contrasted with an earlier time, our young people now are less trusting, especially of those in positions of authority. They feel controlled by external forces and events to the point where they believe they have little influence over their own destinies. They are less authoritarian and have strong negative feelings toward those who hold authority. They are very independent, often to the point of rebelliousness and defiance. They are more free and uncontrolled in their expression of feelings and impulses. They tend to live in the present and are less concerned about the future. They are self-indulgent. Their moral values are relative rather than absolute. They have a strong sense of identification with their peer and age groups. They have a marked social concern, which often manifests itself in a desire to help the less fortunate. They are more negative toward business, and toward business management in particular; they prefer the professions. They want to contribute less to employing organizations. Finally, related to the decline in motivation to manage, they are less competitive, less assertive, less responsible, and, again, more antagonistic to authority.

Many of these characteristics overlap, but even so it is apparent that there has been a broad spectrum of change. Whether this is viewed as good or bad depends in part on the values of the individual, and also on what objective one has in mind — good or bad relative to what goal. Certainly, if the concern is to maintain the economic system in approximately its present form and at its present level of effectiveness, the changes must be viewed as bad. From the point of view of some other goal they may be irrelevant, or even good.

One of the difficulties in describing human characteristics is that many terms have a strong evaluative quality; they tend to imply a judgment of good or bad. This has proved to be a particular problem in much writing about changes in America's youth. Some authors think these changes are good, some think they are bad, and the terms used by each to describe the same characteristics can differ widely.

The discrepancy has been particularly evident in the case of the previously noted tendencies toward independence, free expression, and self-indulgence. These characteristics are often described, by people favoring the changes and identifying with those who have changed, as reflecting *self-actualization* and growth — the emergence of a "higher order" motive which involves realizing one's true, often creative, potential in all its varied ramifications. Self-actualization means developing one's abilities and capabilities to the fullest, and achieving the true self.

I have not used this term in the foregoing discussion because it implies that such a person is somehow more mature and emotionally healthy than others, something that there is no reason to believe is especially true of the current younger generation. Also, it seems to me impossible to know when the motive of self-actualization is operating and when it is not, because what is the "real" person is difficult to know in advance and can certainly vary from one person to another. Yet the term is used frequently in describing the youth of today. Professor Martin Evans, for instance, of the University of Toronto, considers the increase in self-actualization to be one of the two key changes in today's youth, with the other being the decline in authoritarianism. Because the term is frequently used, it is important to indicate why I have not used it. There seems little doubt that we do have a rise in rebellious independence, impulse expression, and self-indulgence (I use the terms of those who did the research in this area). Whether we also have self-actualization is really unknown at the present time — and may well be unknowable. However, it is apparent that those who use the term in the present context are expressing their approval of the changes that have occurred.

6

Student Activism and Protest

At several points I have linked changes in motivation to manage, and other changes as well, to the rise of student protest. Since the protest movement is one of the most significant new developments to have occurred on campus and in the younger generation, it is essential to develop more fully the nature of its relationship to changing motives, attitudes, and values. The discussion to this point has outlined a threat to the free enterprise system which is essentially internal, stemming from a lack of sufficient executive talent. But student activism poses an external threat as well. The New Left ideology which has permeated the student protest movement is in strong opposition to the values and institutions that perpetuate the present economic system. What is the nature and extent of this threat? How does it relate to the threat posed by what I have called the human constraint?

The Rise of Protest

The 1960s saw a drastic change in the behavior of university students, as well as in their motives and attitudes. The first two years of the decade were an extension of the relatively quiescent

1950s but, starting in 1962, with the peace demonstrations in Washington early in the year and the formation of Students for a Democratic Society during the summer, the pace of student activism and militancy began to quicken. By the fall of 1964, the Berkeley campus of the University of California was faced with large-scale demonstrations, which subsequently spread to most of the larger campuses in the country.

Many writers, including Professor Seymour Lipset, of Harvard University, who is widely considered to be one of the most knowledgeable scholars in the field of student politics, have viewed these activities as transitory, derived from the actions of a small minority, and devoid of relationship to deeper social alterations. Such optimism is attractive, but is difficult to maintain in the face of what is now known about the depth and extent of the changes which have occurred.

It appears from the studies considered in Chapter 5 that the shift in values and motives of the college population dates back at least to the early 1950s, although there is no way of knowing whether motivation to manage was affected that early. The change appears to have accelerated gradually until it was sufficiently pronounced and prevalent to permit the emergence of mass behavior based on it. As Professor Lipset has pointed out, the particular form this behavior took derives from the civil rights activities which preceded it and in which some students participated. The tactics of confrontation and civil disobedience were highly visible and available at that particular time, and this probably accounts for the fact that student attitudes were transformed into student activism when they were.

There are certainly many other types of behavior, including the avoidance of managerial work, which can well derive from changing attitudes and motives. It seems very likely that the student protest in question was a manifestation of this change which occurred as the result of a particular combination of external circumstances, among which the civil rights movement, the war in Vietnam, and the rapid growth of American universities appear to have been most prominent. Accordingly, a decrease in violent protest need not signal a reversal in the process of change which has been going on since the early 1950s. Other behavioral manifestations may appear as external circumstances are altered.

The reduced motivation to manage and other changes found to characterize a large number of students are thus not likely to be the single cause of demonstrations and activism. Groups with similarly low motivation to manage have been identified in other contexts, and have not evidenced the same kind of behavior. On the other hand, such attitudes and motives provide fertile ground for activist leadership to emerge, as well as an environment which will continue to nurture it. By now it is abundantly clear that demonstrations have found strong support in the attitudes of student majorities, and that student unrest is not merely the product of a small, dissident minority.

Student unrest has been attributed to alienating forces in the university and to imperfections in the educational experience. Yet alienation is by no means a new phenomenon on the college campus, and it does not appear to be widespread even today. Richard Peterson, of the Educational Testing Service, has accumulated data indicating that imperfections in the educational experience do not seem to be a major issue in demonstrations.

What does appear to have happened is that more students entering colleges and universities have come with attitudes, values, and motives that differ sharply from those of earlier generations. These new attitudes predispose the individual against authority, large and impersonal organizations, and the Protestant ethic of hard work and individual competition. When such students face the authority of large and complex universities they generate leaders who epitomize the attitudes and motives of the majority, and the path to activism is opened.

In large universities with many formal rules and procedures the new attitudes do not need to be as prevalent or as widespread to produce demonstrations, because the bureaucratization is complete, at least from the vantage point of the new student. In less formalized colleges and universities with less complex structures, a greater student attitude base is needed to produce unrest. Different colleges attract students with differing degrees of activism in their attitudes. Smaller schools which are more informal, such as Swarthmore and Antioch, appear to need a strong attitude base to spawn activism. The very large state universities produce activism even though student's attitudes are more widely spread over the entire spectrum.

Changing Motives and Activist Behavior

There is a marked parallel between what is known about the behavior of campus activists and the changes in motivation to manage that have occurred. The parallel is so close, in fact, that it would be almost impossible not to in some way implicate the motivational changes in the rise of student protest. The changes appear to have provided an attitude base favorable to the emergence of a certain kind of student leadership.

The most prounounced shift in attitude has been in the area of authority relationships. Students have become increasingly negative toward people holding positions of authority and toward the idea of hierarchical authority in human groups and organizations. Since demonstrations have frequently involved confrontations with authority, and on occasion even physical attacks on authority figures, an obvious parallel does exist between the attitude changes identified and the changed patterns of behavior.

Studies of activist students reported by Professors Jeanne Block, Norma Haan, and Brewster Smith, at the Berkeley campus of the University of California, have consistently provided evidence of their basic rebelliousness and restlessness. This does not necessarily imply a tendency toward greater emotional disturbance or emotional illness, however. Research conducted by Professor Larry Kerpelman, of the University of Massachusetts, indicated no difference in the level of emotional adjustment of activists and nonactivists. Nor does there appear to be a difference in intelligence. Neither the contention that the activists are psychological supermen nor the opposite view that they are maladjusted incompetents appears to have a basis in fact. Activism is closely associated with low levels of authoritarianism, however.

The strong emphasis on participatory democracy which permeates the activist movement reflects this view of authority. Leadership is essentially devalued and denied, although it clearly exists to some degree. Meetings typically are open; anyone can come in and express a viewpoint. Decisions are at least ostensibly achieved through consensus, and they are often long in the making. This pattern is not characteristic of the black student groups, which exhibit much more individual leadership and are generally closed to outsiders, but participatory democracy is a major characteristic of all other student protest groups.

The decline we have noted in competitive motivation is also consonant with what is known about student activism. There is a strong tendency for activists to be identified politically with the far left and to oppose a competitive economic system. Clearly, opposition to the American business system stems from a number of causes, but at least one of these is the fact that it is viewed as highly competitive and acquisitive.

Activists tend to identify with the loser and the underdog, rather than with the winner; there is a strong desire to alleviate the oppression of others and to help the needy. The studies reported by Professors Block, Haan, and Smith indicate a very limited commitment to the Protestant work ethic, and little concern with achievement and success. There is a marked rejection of competition in the economic sphere, and in other areas as well.

The sharp reduction in assertiveness, traditionally considered a masculine trait, is reflected in the minimal differentiation of sex roles in the activist movement. Activism is closely associated with women's liberation, gay liberation, and other movements which argue for a merging of "masculine" and "feminine" roles. It is also associated with the hippie alternative and the drug culture, both of which advocate dropping out and escapism, a passive turning in to one's own personal experience rather than an active coping with one's environment. This is not to say that all aspects of the student protest movement exhibit a lack of assertiveness, but major components of it clearly do.

The decrease in sense of responsibility for administrative tasks merges easily with the overall rejection of the managerial aspects of large, formal organizations. Professors Irving Horowitz, of Rutgers University, and William Friedland, of the University of California at Santa Cruz, describe this phenomenon as follows: "Much of the student movement is rebelling against bureaucratic forms of organization, perfected and extended by the older generation, preferring spontaneous 'community' and 'happenings,' wholeness, and a moral laissez-faire (to rules and plans)."

There is considerable evidence from other sources in support of this antibureaucratic trend, although much of it has not been so interpreted. For example, activists have consistently evinced a strong tendency to reject formal religion. The rule-oriented, authority-based nature of much formal religion and the church organizations which perpetuate it appear to be the major culprits.

Similarly, it is the very large and complex universities that have experienced the greatest unrest, and it is these universities that have made the most extensive use of impersonal rules and procedures in dealing with students. Although faculty organization tends to be participative and "academic freedom" is stressed, student-university relations have been highly bureaucratized. Student protests have been directed against much of this, including grading systems, class size, dormitory regulations, required attendance, disciplinary practices, food services, dress rules, faculty promotion and tenure policies, censorship of publications, and housing policies.

Professor Allan Silver reports that half of all Columbia University students wanted to become professors before entering the university, but only one sixth indicated the same career choice during the senior year of college. He interprets this change as reflecting a feeling, with increased exposure in the student role, that large universities are essentially bureaucracies, coupled with a strong desire to avoid that kind of organization in the future.

In addition to university governance, a major set of issues in student demonstrations throughout the country has been the Vietnam War and the draft. Although a number of students have participated in demonstrations because of pacifist values and revulsion against physical violence, these factors seem insufficient to account for the extent and nature of the participation. A major factor in the antiwar demonstrations appears to be a rejection of bureaucratic and authoritarian systems as represented by military organizations. This suggests that the draft, rather than the war itself, has been the major object of discontent, and that antiwar sentiment has represented, for many students, a displacement to a more socially acceptable objective. These students not only did not want to fight in Vietnam, but would really prefer not to enter the armed forces at all. This interpretation is reinforced by the fact that student sentiment against the war did not solidify until the 1967-68 academic year. Samuel Lubell attributes this turn against the war on campus to the revised draft law, which eliminated graduate student deferments and accelerated the drafting of seniors upon graduation.

Student Power

The stability, and perhaps even temporary growth, of power motivation, plus a very limited decline in the desire to be in a distinctive position, represent a striking contrast with the changes in other aspects of managerial motivation discussed. Evidence of strong power motivation within the activist sector, if not the sense of having achieved power, parallels these findings. Activist students have consistently demanded a greater voice in university affairs and greater power over decision-making processes. This has extended beyond the student-university relationship to matters of building construction, investment policy, and company recruiting on campus.

At Columbia University, surveys of student attitudes reported by Allen Barton indicate widespread support for the view that students should exercise more control over university policymaking. Similar results have been obtained at Berkeley and elsewhere. A major source of student unrest throughout the country has been the matter of student participation in, if not control over, campus governance. Student power, as opposed to faculty or administrative power, increased steadily as an issue in demonstrations. The demands advanced indicate a desire to exercise power over many aspects of university operations, not just those directly related to student behavior.

The significance of this strong power motivation, coupled with a desire to move to center stage to perpetuate it, is difficult to interpret against a backdrop of increasingly less favorable attitudes toward authority, competitiveness, assertiveness, and responsibility. In large, complex organizations all of these factors move together; on the campus, they have not. When all move together, power motivation is typically muted and channeled so as to be consistent with organizational goals. The more naked power motivation noted among college students is not so restrained and controlled by other attitudes within the individual. The potential for anarchy would seem considerable.

Comparisons With Activists

Although the students whose motives I have studied appear to be like the activists in terms of changing psychological factors, further analysis suggests that their contribution is much more to the attitude base favorable to protest than to its front lines. In fact, my studies of motivation to manage have focused on student groups that seem to be typically least activist and least likely to be involved in demonstrations.

Unrest has been at very low levels among business students. The surveys conducted by Richard Peterson indicate that these students have less social concern and are less liberal in their attitudes than most other groups of students, particularly those in the liberal arts. Furthermore, business students do have more favorable attitudes toward business and business careers.

Apparently these factors predispose students majoring in business administration against overt participation in demonstrations. This at least is the implication of studies on many campuses. Typical is a comparison, by Professors William Watts and David Whittaker, of students who occupied the administration building on the Berkeley campus of the University of California with students who did not. Business students (and those in engineering, too) were markedly underrepresented in the demonstrating group.

Essentially the same conclusion is obtained when one looks into the research that has been done on faculty attitudes toward student activism and protest. Data reported by Professors Seymour Lipset and Everett Ladd indicate that it is in the social sciences that one finds the greatest faculty support for the students and the greatest actual faculty participation in their demonstrations. With the exception of the field of education, which tends to be intermediate, the professional disciplines are at the other extreme. Relatively few business administration faculty members support the activists, although the rejection is not as complete as in the schools of agriculture. Within all disciplines, it is the younger faculty members who are most likely to approve activism. In the peak discipline of sociology, 81 percent of faculty in their twenties indicate approval of student protests, while in this same field only 55 percent of faculty members over sixty approve.

EXHIBIT 26
Approval of Student Activism by Faculty in Various Fields

Field	Percent Approving
Sociology	71
Psychology	63
Political Science	63
Economics	58
Humanities	56
Education	45
Physical and Biological Sciences	40
Business Administration	29
Engineering	26
Agriculture	19

Adapted from an article by Seymour Lipset and Everett Ladd in the November 1970 issue of *Psychology Today*.

There are other factors, in addition to the major field of study, which indicate that the student groups I have studied contain relatively few activists. Participants in demonstrations tend to be disproportionately female, while the business student groups are largely male. The reported age of demonstrators varies, but the proportion of freshmen and sophomores who are not yet twenty is high. It appears that new arrivals on campus, whether freshmen or transfer students, are most likely to be involved. The business students are concentrated at the junior level and in the twenty-and-over age group; because cross sections were used, new transfer students can be assumed to be a rather small minority of the business students. Finally, the most desired occupation among activists, at least in the early college years, appears to be university teaching. On the one occasion when I inquired about this, with the 1967-68 University of Oregon group, only 5 percent of the students indicated teaching as a career objective, and the majority of these were considering positions below the college level.

Thus, on every dimension where information is available, the business students considered in Chapter 4 prove to be different from those who have become activists and have participated in demonstrations on university campuses. This is not true of the 1972-73 liberal arts student group from the University of Maryland, however. A sizable proportion of these students are social science majors; they also are younger, with a number being freshmen, and the representation of females is much greater than in the business administration groups. It is not surprising that motivation to manage accordingly is much lower in this liberal arts contingent.

The "Small Minority" View of Activism

A number of observers have attributed the rise in student protest to the actions of a small minority. According to this view, the college population as a whole remained relatively unchanged, but a new element was added with the rapid increase in the size of college enrollments, and it is this new element that has been the source of the problem.

To account for the changes in motivation to manage and other characteristics that are known to have occurred, and still hold to this idea of a "small minority," it would be necessary that the change process take the form illustrated in the following chart:

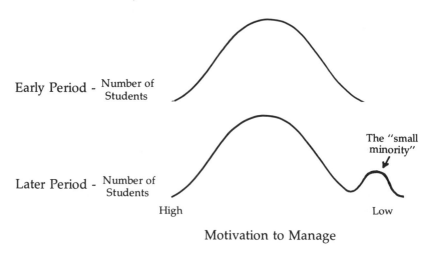

Motivation to Manage

One would expect a greater spreading out of scores in the recent period because of the addition of a group of people with very low motivation, but the proportion with very high levels of motivation should remain roughly unchanged. On the other hand, if the change has been pervasive, one would expect no particular shift in the spread of scores, but the proportion with very high levels of motivation should decline. The change process should take the following form:

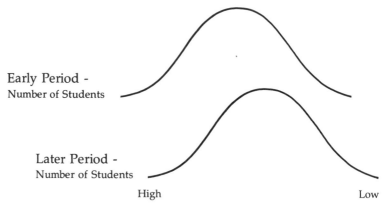

Motivation to manage

In order to determine whether there was a decrease in the percentage of students with very high motivation to manage, and the four aspect motives that changed, the data for the earliest period (1960-61) were split so as to give as close as possible to a 25%-75% break. Then the data for the 1966-67 Portland State University students, the 1967-68 University of Oregon students, and the 1969 University of Maryland students (the three groups studied in the later 1960s) were split at this score established with the 1960-61 data. In every single comparison the proportion of very highly motivated students was lower in the 1966-69 period than in 1960-61. With three comparisons on each of five measures, there were fifteen shifts in one direction and none in the other — something very unlikely to occur by chance. The average decrease in the proportion of students with very high scores was 9 percent.

Statistical analyses were also carried out using the same student groups and the same motives to determine if the spread

---

EXHIBIT 27
Percent of Students With Very High Managerial
Motivation in the Early and Late 1960s
(Motives That Changed)

	Oregon (1960-61)	Portland State (1966-67)	Oregon (1967-68)	Maryland (1969)
Motivation to Manage	22%	11%	14%	15%
Favorable Attitude Toward Authority	15%	10%	7%	11%
Desire to Compete	26%	14%	16%	15%
Assertive Motivation	30%	19%	16%	21%
Sense of Responsibility	27%	17%	19%	20%

of scores had increased meaningfully. On only one of the fifteen analyses, involving the favorable attitude toward authority of the 1969 University of Maryland students, did this prove to be the case. The fourteen other comparisons revealed no meaningful increases.

One must conclude from these analyses, taken as a whole, that the change on the college campuses has been pervasive, and the motivational and attudinal support for activism quite widespread. We cannot write off what has happened as reflecting only the isolated actions of a small minority of troublemakers.

The New Left versus the Human Constraint

Among college students, those whose ideology is on the far left of the political spectrum tend to be much more politically active than any other group. This fact, coupled with the general shift to the left that has occurred among college students, poses a considerable potential threat to the American free enterprise system as it currently exists.

On the other hand, that system has been under external attack from the left for many years. On occasion, as during the Depression of the 1930s, the attack has been mounted in sufficient strength to represent a significant threat. Yet the economic system has remained relatively unaltered in the face of these particular efforts to change it. Furthermore, external attacks of this kind are by nature highly visible, and the business community therefore can take steps to combat them relatively easily.

Given this situation, I cannot view it as likely that the New Left will succeed in producing major changes in the economic system in the foreseeable future — provided, and this is crucial, that the economic system remains productive and its organizations profitable. I very much fear, however, that this will not be the case, for lack of managerial talent needed to produce goods, services, and profits; and thus, to maintain a society and economy of abundance.

If the present economic system fails to provide the American people with the standard of living to which they have become accustomed, then they will change it. This is particularly true of the young Americans who will be in the majority before long and who, as they continue to move through the colleges, will gradually assume control of the country's decision-making processes. The internal sapping of America's economic strength that would result from a generation of ineffective managers, perhaps even very few of these, could produce a degree of weakness sufficient to permit the New Left finally to topple the whole economic structure.

Overall, then, it seems to me that the human constraint imposed by insufficient managerial resources is a much greater threat to this country than that inherent in the rise of the New Left. Yet, if the managerial talent shortage becomes real and its inevitable effects occur, the added problem posed by the New Left cannot be discounted. It becomes imperative, therefore, to find some way of dealing with the need for managerial talent, not only for its own sake, but also to preclude increasing incursions into a softened economic system by the warriors of the New Left.

7

The Roots of Social Change

The three previous chapters have considered parallel changes in motivation to manage and its aspects, changes in other human characteristics, and changes in the extent of student activism. What is needed now is an attempt to integrate these varied findings into a coherent whole. Is it possible to make some general statements, based on these data, regarding the nature of the social change that is occurring? Further, is there any readily available explanation of why the society is undergoing this particular type of change?

In order to answer these questions, it becomes necessary to move away from data and research and to venture in the direction of theory — or, as some may feel, outright speculation. There are some relevant facts that can prove helpful in getting at the roots of the current social change, but they are widely dispersed and it is often a long inductive leap from one to another.

One can legitimately ask what purpose is served by such a foray into the realm of theory, given the limited data available. My answer is that one must obtain the best possible grasp of the full nature of the problem before attempting to develop meaningful solutions. It is clear that a major change has occurred in our society and that certain kinds of motives, attitudes, and values are particularly implicated. But this does not provide a sufficient basis for evaluating various possible alternative ways of dealing with the anticipated managerial talent shortage. For that purpose it is important to have some understanding, no matter how imperfect, of how the processes that initiated change evolved and of the relationships among the different factors involved.

The Central Role of Authority Relationships

The most consistent and pervasive finding from the analyses of change we have seen is that there has been a major disturbance in authority relationships among college students. This finding is in evidence in the studies of motivation to manage described in Chapter 4, in the more diversified studies of Chapter 5, and certainly in the analysis of protest in Chapter 6.

America's youth is becoming more negative to authority, less trusting of authority, less desirous of exercising authority, less accepting of the legitimacy of authority, more rebellious and defiant of authority, less tolerant of authority, less accepting of the moral values held by established authority, and more opposed to organizations viewed as authoritarian, and its behavior is frequently in opposition to existing authority. The decline in motivation to manage can be viewed as reflecting a rejection of the authority role in organizations. Youth's strong ties to peer and age groups appear frequently to be associated with a pulling together or coalescing against authority. There has been an increase in the freedom with which feelings and impulses are expressed, and a greater self-indulgence; here, too, there is a sense of breaking away from controls, and often the uncontrolled expression is in defiance of, or in opposition to, authority.

There are some apparent contradictions in this constellation of authority-related factors, but on further consideration it appears that these can be reconciled. The fact that those who are angry at or hate authority may not trust it is not too surprising. Those in authority may well retaliate, and therefore it is important to be on guard against the prospect of a counterattack. This would seem to be the essence of distrust. One expects to be "hurt" back; or sometimes the sequence gets confused and authority is viewed *a priori* as oppressive and inhuman, which then becomes justification for open attacks on authority.

It also is true that individuals who harbor strong feelings of anger and resentment against authority rarely desire to hold positions of authority themselves. To do so would mean assuming the role of being hated. In part these individuals anticipate that those over whom authority is exercised will resent it, just as they resented the same authority in others. In part there is a hatred of themselves in the new and uncomfortable role of authority figure, which is what is commonly meant by feeling guilty. I have frequently found that people with low motivation to manage are plagued with strong feelings of guilt about performing certain types of managerial tasks. There is thus good reason why members of the current college generation who have strong negative feelings toward authority do not want to manage or exercise authority either.

Authority, Guilt, and Humanism

This formulation, based on the assumption of a widespread disturbance in authority relationships, serves to explain a number of the changes in student attitudes unearthed through research. It does not yet explain the changes in social concern and other factors which, taken together, are best described as a shift in the direction of a more humanistic approach to life and work. It also leaves still unexplained the increased sense of being controlled by external events described by Professor Rotter. I believe these additional changes are best understood as reflecting the feeling of guilt which often accompanies rebellion against authority.

Psychiatrists and clinical psychologists long have noted the close association between anger against authority figures and feelings of guilt. Although the two are certainly not inseparable, they do travel together quite often. Thoughts and behavior viewed as representing attacks on appropriate, legitimate authority elicit a feeling of being bad and deserving of punishment. This guilt is often extremely unpleasant, and people develop a variety of techniques for avoiding it.

One approach, of course, is to contend that the authority is not legitimate; that it is oppressive, unfair, hypocritical, criminal, or anything else which would shift the blame and alleviate the individual's guilt. Another approach is to contend one is really not responsible for one's own behavior. If a person is completely at the mercy of external forces, then how can he be blamed for his defiance of authority? It seems to me not at all surprising that a generation which is increasingly in rebellion against authority should increasingly describe itself as not responsible for its behavior. To present a picture of oneself as powerless in the grip of external forces is a very effective method of pleading "not guilty."

Another approach to avoiding guilt is to lose oneself in a crowd, on the assumption that if so many people are involved in the attack on authority it cannot be wrong. The working of this defense against guilt can be observed frequently in mass demonstrations, and accounts for the frequently observed fact that individuals will do things with a crowd that they will not do alone. The approach is clearly evident in campus protest activities, and would seem to account for the increasing sense of togetherness among the young. If a whole generation is in this together, then how can it be wrong?

Finally, one can deny the guilt, by presenting oneself as a basically good person — tolerant, loving, helpful to the less fortunate, considerate of others. This is the approach which appears to have generated the increasing social concern and humanism of the young. In this context it is important to reemphasize that this reaching out to others does not include those in positions of established authority. It is directed either to "mankind" in the abstract or to the less fortunate. It seems to say, "How can a person, a group, a generation that is so good and concerned for others have done anything that is really bad?" This approach can, of course, easily evolve into an actual identification with the oppressed and the underdog, in an effort to expiate sins and atone for the wrong that has been done. This latter process would have to be considered a more extreme reaction to the guilt aroused by increasing opposition to authority.

It is important to recognize that struggles of the kind described, with their seemingly inevitable circularity of anger and guilt, are not necessarily pathological or unique to the mentally ill. They are part of all human experience to some degree. It is unfortunate that the young appear to have become increasingly entangled in this particular emotional web, however. The possibility that the social concern, and the social work, of the young may stem from underlying psychological processes which appear more self-serving than altruistic need not make them any less praiseworthy. A businessman who contributes an important product or service to society is not less deserving of credit for his contribution because he makes it out of a desire for personal profit.

Disturbed Authority Relationships and Managing

How might these problems of authority, anger, and guilt relate to managing and managerial talent shortages? What can be expected of a generation that seems to be struggling with such problems to a much greater extent than have previous generations?

I have already noted that assuming a managerial position can mean self-hatred and the anticipation of hatred from others in a person who typically experiences strong antiauthority feelings. Among those who have learned to associate such unpleasantness with managerial work, the answer may well be the choice of some other career, perhaps one of the professions where such problems are less likely.

However, there are many who no doubt will end up managing for some period of time. They may not be aware of the difficulties their attitudes toward authority will create for them, or there may be strong forces, such as family pressures, which at least temporarily override any anticipated unpleasantness. From what is known about the ways the young are attempting to cope with guilt, one can piece together a picture of some of the problems they may experience in managing, and the approaches they may take to resolve them.

One approach would be to deny the legitimacy of one's own authority, thus essentially abdicating while continuing officially to hold the position. Such a manager is often described as using a *laissez-faire* managerial style. Managers of this kind are not usually considered very effective.

Another approach would be to portray oneself as being at the mercy of overwhelming forces, such as higher authority or governmental constraints. Because he must ward off guilt by maintaining the image of external control, such a manager is unable to initiate anything on his own. He certainly will contribute little to growth and change in his company.

Another approach is to adopt participative democracy with a vengeance. The manager loses himself in the crowd, often with repeated protestations of the value of "participative management." Authority is transferred to the group, of which the manager is "just another member," and thus guilt is transformed into a sense of having done the right thing. The group may never reach a decision, or it may make a poor one from the viewpoint of company success, but the manager has avoided the guilt of authority.

Finally, there is an approach which involves convincing oneself and others that one is really a good person in spite of one's authority, or perhaps attempting to atone for the "sin" of managing by identifying with the less fortunate. Such a manager may become extensively involved in community action, and these activities may assume much greater importance than profits, so that company resources in sizable quantities are devoted to them. In the ultimate, management may literally give the company away.

I believe that these approaches — *laissez-faire,* paralysis of initiative, excessive participation, and social action at the expense of profit — will almost certainly be among the major problems for management in the future. This seems inevitable as the guilt that is a product of hating authority travels from the college campus to the shop floor, sales territory, and office landscape, and ultimately into the boardroom itself.

Roots of Change: The Evidence From Achievement Motivation

An explanation of how this disturbance in authority relationships came about is difficult to find. The subject of social change has long been of interest to social scientists, but solid knowledge in the area is not extensive. One of the few exceptions is provided by a series of studies conducted under the direction of Professor David McClelland, of Harvard University.

Professor McClelland has been doing research related to achievement motivation since the 1940s. It has become increasingly apparent that the achievement motive he is concerned with is closely related to successful entrepreneurship, the building of economic enterprises. Companies headed by men with strong achievement drives have been found to grow much more rapidly than those which are not. It has also been demonstrated that the sons of entrepreneurs tend to have more achievement motivation than the sons of men in nonentrepreneurial occupations.

While achievement motivation and managerial motivation certainly are not the same things, they do appear to be parallel and sometimes overlapping concepts, both of which have considerable significance for the economic welfare of modern societies. It is for this reason that Professor McClelland's findings regarding the role of achievement motivation in social change and the sources of change concern us here. They provide a useful bridge to my own thinking regarding the roots of the profound alterations in American society that we are experiencing.

Using techniques of historical analysis, Professor McClelland has shown a close association between the level of achievement motivation in a society and its level of economic development. As the achievement drive increases, the economy begins to grow and expand. Typically, in the societies of the past, the level of achievement motivation eventually peaked and started to decline, and a decline in economic accomplishment did not lag far behind. I would assume that in the managerial societies of today, with their dependence on very large economic organizations, motivation to manage would play at least as important a role in this economic cycle as achievement motivation. In any event, the important point is that certain motives do appear to affect economic activity, and that when these motives became scarce in societies of the past, the societies experienced severe economic difficulties; most of them eventually disappeared, at least in their original, successful form.

A second major finding of the research on achievement motivation has to do with its origins. It is clear that what happens in the early family situation is critical. Achievement motivation is transmitted from generation to generation because parents teach it to their children. They teach them that independent mastery of challenges in the world around them is good, and they help them to learn to achieve on their own and to obtain satisfaction from doing so.

Now, what about the United States? Professor McClelland presents data indicating that achievement motivation rose rapidly during the 1800s, and reached a peak around the turn of the century. Of the time since, he says, ". . . achievement concern . . . has decreased more or less regularly, although there is a possibility that the decline has leveled off in the past 30 years. We are still above average and in fact we're at approximately the same level as Russia in 1950, although we were probably on the way down while they were certainly on the way up." This picture of declining achievement motivation, combined with my evidence of decreasing motivation to manage, is not reassuring.

Furthermore, Professor McClelland contends that the source of decline in a society is some kind of break in the process of achievement training so that the motive is no longer transmitted from parent to child. He considers the advent of slavery associated with affluence, such as occurred in ancient Rome, a major factor in accounting for the failure to perpetuate achievement motivation. Slaves take over the child-rearing chores and, being low on achievement motivation themselves, do not inculcate it in the children.

I believe that some such break in the value- and motive-transmission process has occurred in American society, and that this accounts in part for the changes which have occurred in motivation to manage and, more broadly, in authority relationships in general. On the other hand, it is clear that the advent of slavery is not the source of the break, although affluence may well be implicated in other ways.

The Break in Value Transmission

There are a number of factors which appear to have operated in a manner analogous to slavery to disrupt the value-transmission process in American society. Some presumably have operated in one context, some in another, but the cumulative impact appears sizable.

One factor that is related to affluence is the advent of technology and mechanization in the home. A high proportion of families have simply not had to teach work-related values at home, because the total amount of work to be done there has decreased to the point where heavy involvement of children is not necessary. A major exception, however, appears to be those families that conduct a family enterprise to which the children must contribute their share of time and effort. The largest remaining societal sector of this type is the farm population. Not surprisingly, the children of farm parents are least likely, by a sizable margin, to participate in demonstrations on campus. I have noted previously that faculty support for student activism is lowest in schools of agriculture. But it is also true that the number of farm families has been declining for many years.

One consequence of this removal of work from the home environment appears to be a reduction in the extent to which children are exposed to, and thus learn to cope with, the demands of adult authority. This, of course, is particularly true of authority in the work sphere, where we find some of the greatest problems today.

A factor that has received relatively little attention to date, probably in part because society has embraced women's liberation with such enthusiasm, is the increasing number of working mothers who spend less time at home, and thus have less time to spend transmitting values. The trend toward increased labor force participation by women has occurred at the same time that many fathers are engaged in increasing amounts of travel and thus are away from home for longer and longer periods of time. It is not at all unlikely that babysitters, day care centers, and other parent-substitutes can play much the same role in contributing to a break in value transmission as slavery did in societies of the past. The parent-substitutes may well lack either the desire or the ability to teach parental values.

The initial impetus to the increased employment of women came during the manpower shortages of World War II. Female labor force participation rates have never since returned to pre-war levels. However, as Howard Hayghe, of the U. S. Bureau of Labor Statistics, points out, "Before the 1960's the number of wives under 35 in the labor force rose relatively slowly . . . Between 1966 and 1972, the increase in the number of wives under 35 in the labor force outpaced that of older wives." Data for working wives with children at home follow a similar pattern. Thus, the full impact of increasing labor force participation by mothers appears to lie ahead. Whether this factor had a truly significant role in the changes on campus during the 1960s is open to some question.

In all probability, neither mechanization of the home nor the departure of parents has been as instrumental for change as a third factor, the widespread embracing of a highly permissive approach to rearing children, particularly in the more affluent and intellectual sectors of society. Permissiveness, with its failure to use punishment and discipline, can mean that attitudes, values, and motives are developed quite independent of parental influence. Society's values are thus transmitted less forcefully because parents often stop consciously transmitting values at all, and may, in fact, make a determined effort *not* to transmit values, on the theory that children should develop their own. In this vacuum other influences may take over and a new value system may emerge, thus yielding major social change.

That one result of this process is a disturbance in authority relations seems highly predictable. Because they grow up having little experience with authority, children have no opportunity to learn how to cope with it. Some may have no meaningful conception of what formal, appropriate authority really is. Later on, when they come into contact with the authority systems of large organizations, they are frustrated, confused, and end by forming strong negative attitudes, with results like those considered earlier in this chapter. Professor Kenneth Keniston, of Yale University, notes that ". . . most entering Freshmen have extremely high hopes regarding the freedom of speech and action they will be able to exercise during college. Most of them . . . graduate thoroughly disabused of their illusions."

In many cases this process may be supplemented with another in which rebellion against authority becomes manifest at an earlier age. Angered by the failure of their permissive parents to provide some structure for their lives and to help them with the problems they face, children can develop strong negative feelings toward their parents, feelings which are subsequently transferred to other authority figures and in fact to everything that is viewed as reflecting authority.

One might expect that under conditions where parents are highly permissive, guilt would not develop in relation to antiauthority attitudes and behavior, and thus that in later life the coupling of anger and guilt would not appear. Clinical experience does not support this assumption, however, and in fact it indicates just the opposite. When children become angry at permissive parents (and all children become angry at their parents sometimes), they tend to experience more guilt than they would if the parents were highly punitive. Permissive parents typically present themselves to their children as very concerned about the child's welfare and development, and thus as altruistic and unselfish. Such parents are likely to be perceived by the children as basically good people, incapable of doing wrong. The full weight of guilt, therefore, falls on the child. In contrast, more punitive parents are likely to be viewed as indulging in excesses, and accordingly as bad. The child, although frequently angry, may well be saved from feelings of guilt because it is so clear to him that the blame belongs elsewhere.

It is important to recognize that the philosophy of permissiveness came primarily from educators, and is, therefore, certainly no less prevalent in the schools than among parents. It dates back at least to the progressive education theories advocated by John Dewey in writings published around the time of World War I and for many years thereafter. Professor Dewey's influence on developing conceptions of the educational process, emanating from Columbia University, was tremendous. Somewhat later Dr. Benjamin Spock and a number of child psychologists were to have a similar influence when they presented the doctrine of permissiveness to parents. Because of this dual impact, in both home and school, deficiencies in learning to deal with authority appear to have achieved an unusual pervasiveness. The child did not learn about authority when he left home and went to school, since the situation was much the same there, particularly in the lower grades.

There may well be other factors that have contributed to the break in the value-transmission process, but the coalescing of just these three — less work to be performed at home, less time at home for both mothers and fathers, and a more permissive attitude on the part of both parents and teachers — seems adequate to account for major social change. All three appear to have started slowly, sometime prior to or during World War II, and to have grown since, although at somewhat differing rates; all can now be said to be in a period of rapid acceleration.

The Family Backgrounds of Student Activists

A number of studies have been conducted which examine the upbringing of student activists. These studies introduce another set of factors into our consideration of the roots of change, although the new factors apply only to the individuals who are at the forefront of change. At this point it becomes clear that what has happened is far from being the consequence of some single determinant; a number of different family constellations appear to have come together at a point in time to produce a significant social change. What they have in common is the potential for contributing to a major disturbance in authority relationships.

Apparently, many of the very early activists on the Berkeley campus of the University of California were in chronic rebellion against their parents and most other sources of authority. However, data marshalled by Professor Richard Flacks, of the University of Chicago, make it evident that this has not been the subsequent pattern.

Most activists come from relatively high-income families, and their parents are college graduates. The parents tend to be employed in occupations of an intellectual or professional nature, but rarely in business. The mothers often work. In political ideology the parents are typically quite liberal. A not inconsequential minority are on the extreme left of the political spectrum — radicals or socialists. Yet, overall, the parents are not as radical as their activist children.

Although the parents did adopt many permissive practices in rearing their children (we might expect these to be families, for instance, in which children were permitted to talk back to their parents at the dinner table), this was not true in all respects. When it came to intellectual and social values, the parents of activists made a conscious effort to influence their children. In general they were in complete sympathy with the subsequent activist activities of their children, holding similar attitudes themselves toward business organizations and institutionalized authority. The homes are described as ". . . democratic, egalitarian, and anti-authoritarian" in atmosphere. "The traditional domination of the father is likely to be totally absent."

Taken as a whole, the research seems to indicate that among those at the forefront of campus protest, antiauthority attitudes and the various manifestations of humanism may well have been actively taught in the home, and that relationships with parents as authority figures are likely to be quite serene. Here there has been no break in the value-transmission process, relationships with parents are supportive, and guilt may well be less. On the other hand, the values transmitted clearly are not those of the dominant American culture. I suspect that the capacity to exhibit overt activist behavior and to lead others in such behavior reflects the security inherent in this knowledge of parental support.

Converging Forces

It seems highly unlikely to me that the changes in our society are a reflection of anything other than revised patterns of child-rearing; however, I do believe that several such patterns, each quite different, have converged to produce the present result; there is no single such source. I have tried to trace some of the roots that seem most obvious to me. There may well be others, although I suspect that this analysis has dealt with most of the causes that have contributed to the new attitudes, values, and motives.

I will draw upon this discussion at various points in Part II, in considering a number of approaches that society, particularly its economic organizations, might take to offset or eliminate the problems ahead. Until now I have predicted an inevitable crunch in managerial talent and an inevitable "decline and fall" for our existing society. However, things may not be quite so bad, and the problems not quite as insurmountable as they seem.

Part II

What Can Be Done?

8

Managerial Manpower Planning and the Search for Strategies

The problem that has been posed is important for American society as a whole, not merely for certain of its constituent organizations. In the past, human resource problems or potential problems often have elicited massive federal programs with sizable governmental expenditures. Although this approach, at a level involving the entire society, might well provide solutions to the impending executive talent shortage, it seems unlikely that it will be undertaken. The prospect of the government's investing large sums of money directly into the management of the country's large corporations, thereby making profits greater and stockholders richer, is difficult to imagine. Any federal administration that attempted to do so would in all likelihood be committing political suicide, especially given the values of the younger generation.

In the past, interventions of this kind have occurred only when a single firm whose continued operation is clearly vital to the national welfare has been on the brink of disaster. Perhaps later, should the problems of managerial talent reach crisis proportions and be clearly evident to all, governmental action might become palatable to the electorate; for the present we must look to other types of solutions.

The difficulty stemming from political repercussions is compounded by the fact that the same changes in values, motives, and attitudes that contribute to problems in staffing managerial positions have positive implications for other occupational areas. Professions such as teaching and the law should benefit; in fact they may well be flooded with more outstanding talent than they can possibly absorb. To the extent that low managerial motivation contributes to success in scientific research, we can anticipate increasing numbers of outstanding researchers in the younger generation. It is thus very difficult to convince many people that the social change we are experiencing poses a major threat to society's survival. Unless people recognize the crucial role played by the economic sector and the need for capable management, they are likely to view the changes of the past few years as having primarily positive implications.

Sweeping the Problem Under the Rug

Given the widespread indifference toward, or perhaps even outright political opposition to, any coordinated managerial manpower program at the national level, I see no alternative at present to looking to the individual organizations affected for solutions. Large organizations, and in particular business organizations, will have to recognize and then solve their own problems. If enough of them do, society's problem will be solved as well.

This requires first and foremost that the problem be clearly recognized. There is a real possibility, however, that some companies, perhaps even many, may not do so, or may see the problem only after its effects have weakened the organization beyond repair.

What can happen is that a company will attract people into its managerial jobs by paying sizable amounts of money and offering a host of other attractive inducements. People may join a firm, not to manage, but to obtain many other things that they want. They are induced to stay by the fact that very little is required of them, especially very little real managing. Furthermore, the standards used in connection with management-appraisal systems or other performance-evaluation procedures are revised downward so that the new "managers" appear to be just as effective as the former ones.

This process may well permeate an organization very gradually; each year the company gives more and is managed less, while performance standards drop another notch. There is no apparent managerial talent shortage because all positions are filled and the regular evaluation procedures that have been used for years indicate that management "is just as good as it used to be." There is no burgeoning of ineffective performance because appraisal systems have been adjusted so that it cannot become evident.

Yet in spite of the lack of apparent problems in the area of managerial staffing and performance, profits drop and ultimately the company rots away. It loses out to other firms in its industry. Ultimately a whole American industry may disappear as foreign competition takes over.

This result may occur without anyone's consciously attempting to hide the problem posed by declining will to manage in the organization. The problem has a persistent tendency to creep under the rug all by itself, with very little sweeping by anyone. Thus, there has to be a concerted *effort* to identify such problems, if managerial talent shortages are to be clearly recognized. It is not enough to sit back and assume that if problems of this kind exist, they will immediately become manifest by themselves. They may appear only in the form of their consequence, declining competitive position, and that may occur only after some period of time.

Managerial Manpower Planning

In conceptualizing the managerial talent shortage problem at the company level, it is helpful to think in terms of manpower planning. This process seeks to ensure that the right numbers and kinds of people will be at the right places at the right times in the future, capable of doing those things necessary to the continued achievement of organizational goals. At the managerial level this is done by

    (a) forecasting future needs for mangers;

    (b) making an inventory of existing managerial resources;

    (c) projecting present resources into the future and comparing the anticipated future managerial manpower position against the needs that have been forecast; and

    (d) planning the personnel activities required to meet future managerial manpower requirements.

In forecasting future needs for managers, company growth is a major consideration. Given an expanding economy, a sizable number of companies will grow into new markets and extend product lines. Thus most companies would forecast an increasing demand for managerial talent over the next five or ten years, or at least a stable demand. Very few would anticipate a decline.

Inventories of existing managerial resources typically take into account not only the number and level of current managers, but their present performance and potential for future advancement as well. Thus, an attempt is made to determine whether performance in the position now held is up to the level needed, and also whether the manager could be expected to perform capably in various positions above him, now or at some time in the future. If this process is solidly tied to some standardized benchmark of accomplishment, such as profit performance, it can provide useful protection against failure to identify managerial talent shortages because of gradually eroding standards.

In all probability current inventories of managerial talent are entirely adequate in a number of firms. Some companies report unfilled positions, but some have developed a sizable backlog of managerial talent, and in certain larger corporations early retirement of competent managers is often permitted, even encouraged. Although few companies would deny a desire for even higher caliber personnel and certain firms do indicate some shortages, especially at the level of general management, present supply appears adequate to the demand in a number of others. The vanguard of the new generation have not yet reached an age when a very large number would be expected to assume real managerial responsibility in large corporations.

It is when these supplies are projected five to ten years into the future that the problem of managerial talent shortages appears on something approaching a universal basis. The usual number of voluntary quits, retirements (perhaps increasingly at full term, rather than early), firings, and deaths can be anticipated. But the people coming along to fill the managerial positions left vacant, and new ones created, are not equal either in numbers or in performance potential to those who will have departed. Thus a gap will gradually appear between the demand for fully qualified managers and the supply available. The supply will drop, and it can be expected to continue to drop over at least a ten-year period, even if our society should suddenly experience a massive reversal of past trends and the will to manage unexpectedly return to the campus. It is much more likely that the gap will continue to widen. Any meaningful managerial manpower planning system, using currently accepted practices, would have to project a widening gap over the full term of the forecast, be it five, ten, or even twenty years.

It is the value of an effective manpower planning system

that it does permit a clear recognition of the managerial talent shortage problem through an analysis of anticipated supply-and-demand relationships. It serves to keep the problem from disappearing under the rug. Furthermore, it sets the stage for developing the necessary personnel strategies so that in fact the gap between supply and demand never does emerge; instead the organization prospers and continues to achieve its goals.

Developing Strategies

In evaluating the various strategies that might be planned and introduced to prevent a managerial talent shortage, it may be helpful to work from a model or paradigm which views the different approaches in a systems context. In the systems view, the "input" is people, with their various motives, aptitudes, and capabilities. The "output" is performance, in the present case managerial performance, which leads to the achievement of organizational objectives and goals. "Mediators," or the factors which may intervene between input and output to influence performance, are such things as training, the actions of superiors, definitions of job requirements, pay, and the like.

When searching for strategies to solve human resource problems, I have often found it helpful to look separately at the processes that relate to input, output, and the mediators. These three types of processes are sufficiently differentiated one from the other that they require independent consideration, and frequently also require that independent organizational components undertake them.

The input-related processes are concerned with locating potential employees for a given type of work, deciding which candidates would in all probability contribute most to the company, and finally, inducing these individuals to accept employment. These recruiting and selection procedures are much the same for managers as for nonmanagers, although there are sizable differences in the relative emphasis on the techniques and recruiting sources utilized. Strategies for handling anticipated managerial shortages via the input route involve finding people with management potential and inducing them to enter upon managerial careers.

In contrast, mediator-based strategies involve either changing people after hiring to make them capable of performing more effectively as managers, or adjusting the way the work is organized to fit the capabilities of available personnel. Strategies for filling managerial talent needs through the use of mediators would involve such approaches as management development, executive compensation systems, organization development, and organization planning.

Management Appraisal

I will consider the pros and cons of various input processes and mediators in the chapters which follow. A number of these approaches require extended discussion because they appear, at least on the surface, to provide inherently attractive solutions, and they need to be evaluated in terms of the available research to see if they really can be expected to succeed.

In contrast, a primary reliance on output processes is not nearly as inherently attractive. In fact, as a strategy it appears to be totally inconsistent with the idea of talent shortages. It is a strategy to be used in times of talent abundance rather than scarcity.

An output-based strategy places primary emphasis on the evaluation of performance in management positions, with a view to weeding out those who fail. There is relatively little emphasis on developing procedures for predicting who will be a good manager and finding the types of people needed (input-based strategy); nor are mediators such as management development given much attention. It is assumed that business schools or colleges will provide the company with people who have at least a fair chance of proving themselves as managers, and self-development is viewed as an individual responsibility. Thus the major emphasis in the output-based strategy is placed on continuous evaluation of present managers, using a management-appraisal system of one kind or another. Typically, profit performance is an inherent aspect of the appraisal process.

This is the type of delayed selection that many companies have used in the past, and that many are still using today. Actual on-the-job performance as a manager is assessed to determine whether the person is one the company wants to employ on a continuing basis; often this decision is reevaluated throughout the manager's career. Employment may be terminated at any point if performance does not measure up to expectations. Often standards are set at very high levels and therefore a great many terminations occur. I know of one instance where a firm has maintained a ratio of one person retained for every six hired over a period of many years.

This is a "sink or swim" strategy, typically combined with an "up or out" policy and the use of profit centers. It works well when the company has access to an almost unlimited supply of potential managers and when close attention is given to the performance-evaluation process. Usually those who survive are paid very well, have a sense of accomplishment and elitism, and are good managers, proven under fire. This has been a very appealing approach. It represents a transposing of the American dream from the individual entrepreneur to the manager of large-scale enterprise. It emphasizes individual drive, and where these characteristics are found it has worked.

The difficulty is that this output emphasis assumes an abundance of human resources comparable to the abundance of natural resources in the United States during the period when the output strategy flourished. The developing American economy burned up resources, both human and material, at an alarming rate, but it did not matter because there was always more available. As long as the net that is cast for new managerial talent brings in a sufficient number who survive and prosper, it does not matter that many do not. One can always cast the net again.

But when the number who "swim" (or at the very least "tread water") is small, when the net has to be cast repeatedly and even then cannot keep up with the outflow of those who "sink," when the failure rate becomes excessive, then this output approach is no longer valid. Managerial positions at lower levels are not adequately staffed and few good managers are available for movement upward. Considering that individuals with little motivation to manage are more likely to fail in managerial jobs and that the number of such individuals is increasing sharply, the conditions necessary for an output-strategy emphasis to succeed are rapidly disappearing. The company that stays with this approach alone is likely to be left far behind, and eventually will experience the full impact of the executive talent shortage. There simply will not be sufficient executive talent in each random sample of applicants hired to meet the demand.

In fact, companies known to be using an output strategy may find themselves even worse off for management talent than a random sampling of managerial job candidates across the country would suggest. One of the aspects of managerial motivation that has been declining rapidly is competitiveness. A company that presents an image strongly emphasizing individual competition among managers may completely "turn off" the younger generation. A great many will not even consider working for such a firm. Thus the strategy that calls for the largest number of people to be hired for placement in management positions operates at the same time to attract the smallest number of candidates, given the current character of the managerial labor pool.

Strategies for Small Businesses and Professional Firms
I should stress that what has been said about output processes

applies only to larger companies. In fact, this caveat holds for all of the strategies to be considered in ensuing chapters. In the smaller firm with, say, less than 300 employees, it is generally agreed that the will to manage is of less importance. The character of the chief executive typically can permeate the whole organization because it is so small, and it is his entrepreneurial drive or achievement motivation, rather than his motivation to manage, that appears to have the greater impact on company success.

Furthermore, because it is small and thus has a limited need for new managerial talent in any event, the small business may be able to utilize an output strategy successfully where a larger firm could not. It is one thing to try to identify one really good manager each year, and quite another to attempt to identify 500.

An output strategy may also work well in professional organizations, most of which tend to be relatively small as well. In firms made up primarily of professionals such as lawyers or accountants, motivation to manage appears to have little significance. I suspect that professional loyalties, standards, norms, and ethics serve much the same role in guiding behavior and maintaining commitment to the goals of the organization that managerial authority does in a large corporation. Thus managing and motivation to manage are less likely to be needed.

In addition, while the talent pool of effective managers is dwindling, that of effective professionals is expanding. Given the abundance of human resources available, I would think professional firms might do well to utilize policies like "sink or swim" or "up or out." The labor market is at an appropriate point for such a strategy, or at least it will be before long.

The Older Manager and Retirement Policies

Within many larger companies there still is considerable time before the managerial talent shortage becomes a crucial reality, time which can be used to develop strategies for coping with the problem. For a number of firms it will be five years at least before the situation becomes acute.

During this period these companies can rely primarily on older managers. The grace period can even be stretched by moving to a flexible retirement policy which permits effective managers to stay on, perhaps even encourages them to do so. Instead of pushing everyone out at some specified age such as sixty-five, or in some cases sooner if early retirement is invoked, flexible retirement places the retirement date at the point when the manager can no longer make a meaningful contribution to the company. It is thus highly individualized.

This is the one situation where an output-process emphasis does become meaningful for the large corporation in relation to the managerial talent crunch. As managers become older, probably from age fifty-five on, it is important to monitor their performance to determine if physical and psychological factors associated with advancing age are taking an undue toll. Repeated appraisals are called for. Many managers can continue to function effectively well into their seventies. The will to manage continues undiminished, and they are aided by increasing wisdom and often increasing intelligence as well. Certainly most managers have a good three to five years of performance capability left at the time they retire, and many can be induced to use it if necessary. Thus, the talent shortage can be temporarily stayed, and additional time for planning solutions obtained.

Yet eventually even these managers will retire and the string will run out. It is clearly time to start planning in order to avoid the need for very costly and probably fruitless crisis-based action in the future. There is no aspect of manpower planning and human-resources strategy formulation that demands more attention at the present time than the matter of managerial talent.

9

New Sources of Talent

From the company viewpoint an obvious approach to the problem of talent shortages is to try to attract and retain as many young people as possible who do have the kind of knowledge, the intelligence, and most important of all the motivation that contribute to management potential. It is evident that because of changing motivational patterns the pool of such individuals is shrinking. However, if most companies do *not* make an effort to identify people who possess the needed motives, the companies that do make the effort should be able to skim the top off the existing labor market rather easily.

This approach, of course, is going to be most helpful to the firms that start using it first, and some already are. It tends to produce a few well-managed companies and a great many that are not. Its contribution to solving the overall problem for American society is limited, as it concentrates scarce managerial resources in a few companies.

The critical features of this type of input-process strategy include the widespread recruiting of managerial candidates, the use of some technique to identify managerial motivation within this candidate pool, inducements to those so identified to join the company, and implementation of whatever policies are necessary to keep the good managers thus obtained from being attracted to other firms. A number of methods of identifying motivation to manage are available, including the psychological scales used in the research reported in Chapters 2, 3, and 4 and several other psychological measures of motives, attitudes, and interests which have been shown to bear a relationship to motivation to manage.

The success of this input-process strategy will depend to a large extent on the degree of public awareness of the shortages ahead. Stockpiling managerial talent against future shortages requires an increased investment in recruiting. In the past, a hundred candidates might have produced twenty good prospects; under conditions of declining motivation to manage the same one hundred candidates might produce only ten, or even only five, top prospects. This means that recruiters may need to come up with two hundred candidates, or even four hundred, merely to retain previous talent levels. Furthermore, inducing these individuals to join the company, and to stay, will require at the very least some very healthy starting salaries, as well as attractive raises at frequent intervals.

The approach described makes sense as long as not too many companies recognize that they are faced with managerial talent shortages or as long as not too many companies use this particular approach to deal with the talent shortage. But when the problem becomes widely recognized, supply and demand differentials inevitably will tend to bid up costs to the point where the strategy becomes less and less effective. Initial salaries for individuals who exhibit executive talent can be expected to rise sharply; salaries paid for purposes of retention can become prohibitive. Many companies already have experienced this phenomenon as a result of the scramble for talented members of minority groups, occasioned by federal activities related to civil rights and fair employment practices.

At least for the next few years this input strategy should prove workable for the limited number of companies that attempt to use it. A great many other companies simply will not realize that there is a problem ahead, or will decide to deal with it when it arrives. Some employers may not be able effectively to mobilize their resources to implement the strategy, even though they wish to. Thus, the companies that do move to stockpile managerial talent will at the very least buy valuable time in which to plan and implement other strategies. In some cases this may supplement the time already gained by a move toward flexible retirement.

Tapping New Sources

Ultimately, the strategy of skimming off the cream from existing talent sources will fail, because the number of talented people available will be limited and too many companies will be attempting to attract them. For some companies it will be pointless to try this route because they did not begin early enough. An alternative approach, which also relies heavily on input processes, is to move to new sources of talent, and recruit from segments of the labor force that previously have been utilized only rarely, if at all.

In evaluating such new sources of managerial manpower and developing strategies applicable to them, it is important to be aware of the individual characteristics required for effective managerial performance and of the extent to which these characteristics are likely to be found in various population groups. To date I have focused primarily on managerial motivation because it is that aspect of management potential that is becoming deficient in the population groups from which executive talent has typically been drawn in the past. Now it is time to expand the discussion to include needed characteristics which might prove to be relatively deficient in other population groups that might serve as new sources of managerial talent.

Aspects of Management Potential

A number of studies have been conducted to investigate relationships among motives, attitudes, other psychological traits, and managerial success. The characteristics which emerge most frequently bear a striking resemblence to the aspects of motivation to manage already discussed. Often the characteristics are described in different terms — "dominance" rather than "desire to exercise power," for instance — but the implications are similar.

Two of the most comprehensive analyses of this type were conducted by Professor Thomas Mahoney with Thomas Jerdee and Allan Nash, from the Industrial Relations Center of the University of Minnesota, and Professor Edwin Ghiselli, of the University of California at Berkeley. The former's study dealt with 468 managers in 13 Minnesota firms; the latter's with 306 managers in 90 different companies. In both cases performance ratings by superiors were used as an index of success, and in both cases, also, the measured characteristics most closely associated with the ratings are of essentially the same nature as certain aspects of motivation to manage.

These studies are in agreement in another area as well. In both instances a measure of intelligence proved to be associated with managerial success. In summarizing his conclusions from an extensive review of the research in this area, Professor Ghiselli writes, "For managerial occupations as a whole, measures of intellectual ability would appear to give the best predictions of job proficiency." This statement is based on research studies which utilized a total of more than 5,000 managers. However, Professor Ghiselli did not compare the results obtained from measures of intelligence directly with those from measures of motivation to manage. When such a comparison is made, motivation to manage appears to be an even better predictor of managerial success than intelligence, but not by a great deal.

The importance of intelligence is further emphasized in a study John Culver and I did some years ago. The study dealt with top-level corporate executives, over half of whom were company presidents. The average intelligence in this group fell well within the top 5 percent of the workforce. It appears that one does not reach the top levels of the executive hierarchy, or at least does not survive long there, without being very intelligent.

Research conducted in some of the country's largest corporations repeatedly indicates the importance of intelligence as a component of management potential. Personnel research studies carried out by Douglas Bray and Donald Grant, of American Telephone and Telegraph, in various operating companies of the Bell system, has consistently identified intelligence as a major factor in managerial success. Jon Bentz has found the same thing in studies conducted over many years among managers at Sears, Roebuck. An extensive review of data provided by members of the personnel research unit at Standard Oil of New Jersey leads John Campbell, Marvin Dunnette, Edward Lawler, and Karl Weick to conclude in their book *Managerial Behavior, Performance, and Effectiveness* that intelligence is a major component of management potential in the many components of what is now the Exxon organization.

Intelligence is important in managerial work because it facilitates decision making and planning, the process of reasoning through to a rational course of action. But this process also requires knowledge relevant to the matter under consideration. Thus the particular kind of knowledge or information relating to the decisions a manager must make is also an important ingredient in management potential. Much of this information is specific to the particular functional field of management, such as marketing, industrial relations, or finance; much, too, is specific to a particular industry or even to a given geographical area. It pays, for instance, for a manager to be well informed about the people in the city or region of the country where he conducts business.

It might be expected, from this emphasis on knowledge, that university grades would be highly predictive of subsequent success in management. Yet the relationship proves to be minimal at best, because much of what is learned in school has relatively little direct application to managerial work. Furthermore, what is relevant may well apply to a type of managerial work that is not the same as the managerial career path actually followed, as in the case of a marketing major who spends most of his life in manufacturing management. Then, also, there is a great deal a manager needs to know about his industry, the people he deals with, and the like, that cannot be learned in school.

All in all, the knowledge that is important for effective managerial performance is that which helps in making decisions in the particular job a person holds. Such knowledge comes from a variety of sources, and university training is certainly one of them. Most studies indicate that educational level attained is related to managerial success; furthermore, a kind of education, such as business administration or engineering, that is practically relevant to the job to be done contributes more to management potential than one which is not. However, grade point average across many courses does not appear to be an effective index of the amount of relevant learning.

Management potential, then, appears to be compounded out of a group of factors: motives and attitudes that can be broadly subsumed under the rubric of motivation to manage, intelligence as it contributes to decision making, and the particular information a manager needs to make his decisions. Being broadly educated and knowledgeable in an area such as the humanities, say, is probably of little value for managerial work, although it may personally be highly satisfying in its own right. Subsequent research may well expand this list of factors, but from what is known at present it would appear that management potential means motivation, intelligence, and relevant knowledge.

Women as Managers?

One obvious new source of managerial talent to consider is the female population. While women constitute over 35 percent of the national labor force, they hold only 16 percent of the managerial positions. Although this figure represents a considerable rise above the 12 percent found in 1940, it remains true that women are distinctly underrepresented at the management level.

A survey conducted by Professor Eleanor Schwartz, of Georgia State University, indicates that at least a third of all companies have practically no women in management at all. Banks, insurance companies, and merchandising firms have the most female managers, and the larger firms are more likely to have a sizable female managerial component than the smaller ones. In terms of level, women are most likely to be first-line supervisors or, somewhat less frequently, in middle management; they are almost nonexistent in top management. There is also considerable variation among the different areas of a business, with female managers most prevalent in general administration and production.

A survey by The Bureau of National Affairs, Inc., confirms a number of Professor Schwartz's findings while adding certain additional information. It is evident, for instance, that outside the business sector, in government, hospitals, and the like, where shortages of male managerial talent have long existed, there is a much more extensive use of female managers. Furthermore, within the business world it is the manufacturing companies that have used women least. However, there does appear to have been an increase over the past five years in the number of women in management in all types of organizations. To what extent this has been caused by the pressure of fair employment and equal opportunity laws is not entirely clear.

Reported company experience with women in managerial jobs is definitely favorable. Furthermore, it appears that women succeed as managers for essentially the same reasons that men do — because they possess the will to manage, the intelligence to make decisions, and the necessary knowledge. In my own studies I have repeatedly found that motivation to manage is just as closely related to promotion and successful management-appraisal ratings for women as for men. In a department store, for instance, where over half of the managers are women, the amount of managerial motivation rises steadily as one moves from the lowest level of management, the selling supervisors, to the assistant department managers and finally to the department heads. These female department managers have particularly strong desires to exercise power and to be in distinctive positions.

EXHIBIT 28
Motivation to Manage of Female Managers at Different
Levels in a Department Store

Motivation to Manage	Selling Supervisors	Assistant Managers	Department Managers
High Motivation	9 (33%)	2 (40%)	8 (67%)
Low Motivation	18 (67%)	3 (60%)	4 (33%)
Desire to Exercise Power			
High Motivation	16 (59%)	3 (60%)	10 (83%)
Low Motivation	11 (41%)	2 (40%)	2 (17%)
Desire for a Distinctive Position			
High Motivation	11 (41%)	2 (40%)	7 (58%)
Low Motivation	16 (59%)	3 (60%)	5 (42%)

The Supply of Female Talent

Insofar as the intelligence aspect of management potential is concerned, there is little difference between men and women. Thus, on this particular dimension the female population clearly does offer a major pool of unused managerial talent. On the other hand, women have not been attracted to colleges of business and engineering in anything like the proportions they represent of the overall college student population, and thus, there is a problem in finding women with knowledge relevant to managerial work. In the business student groups that I have been studying since 1960, only about 10 percent are females, and there is some indication that this proportion has been shrinking recently. A number of business schools have discontinued their majors in secretarial science and business education, with the result that the female students who ordinarily selected these majors, and were required to take a broad range of business subjects as a consequence, have shifted to other curricula in the university.

Motivation to manage does not appear to differ to any meaningful extent when male and female managers are studied. In the department store mentioned earlier there was no real difference in overall motivation; the largest difference in a particular aspect was in assertiveness, where the women were clearly lower, a not unexpected finding in view of the association of this measure with masculinity. Other research suggests that in some settings female managers may have less desire for power, but may compensate for this with a more favorable attitude toward authority. In any event, among practicing managers the women can be expected to have just as strong a will to manage as the men, although there may be differences in specific aspects. Thus, from this perspective the talent is there.

A problem is apparent, however, when one looks at the college groups from which future female managers must be drawn. Among business school students the females have considerably lower motivation to manage than the males. This has been a consistent finding in all of the groups that I have studied. The same pattern emerges outside the business school, among liberal arts majors, for example, although it is not present among

EXHIBIT 29
*Motivation to Manage of Male
and Female Managers in a
Department Store*

Motivation to Manage	Male Managers	Female Managers
High Motivation	16 (62%)	27 (61%)
Low Motivation	10 (38%)	17 (39%)
Favorable Attitude Toward Authority		
High Motivation	12 (46%)	28 (64%)
Low Motivation	14 (54%)	16 (36%)
Desire to Compete		
High Motivation	15 (58%)	19 (43%)
Low Motivation	11 (42%)	25 (57%)
Assertive Motivation		
High Motivation	17 (65%)	19 (43%)
Low Motivation	9 (35%)	25 (57%)
Desire to Exercise Power		
High Motivation	11 (42%)	19 (43%)
Low Motivation	15 (58%)	25 (57%)
Desire for a Distinctive Position		
High Motivation	14 (54%)	20 (46%)
Low Motivation	12 (46%)	24 (54%)
Sense of Responsibility		
High Motivation	14 (54%)	26 (59%)
Low Motivation	12 (46%)	18 (41%)

students in the field of education, where male and female students have very similar levels of motivation to manage. This results largely from the fact that females with more such motivation appear to be attracted to school teaching. Having chosen this career, however, and invested time and effort in preparing to follow it, it seems unlikely that many female education majors can be diverted into business management. Female education students, then, are not a likely executive talent source, except for those interested in educational administration.

Among the various aspects of motivation to manage, female college students are particularly lacking in assertive motivation, desire to exercise power, and desire to compete. They tend to have more favorable attitudes toward authority than the males. This suggests that women might be most likely to fail as managers, if they do fail, because they do not take charge and push hard for results and their own advancement. Success would most likely stem from their ability to get along well and avoid conflict in a hierarchical system. Research conducted by Marshall Sashkin and Professor Norman Maier, at the University of Michigan, indicates that when women are placed in positions of authority they are less likely than men to take liberties and to act on their own, unless they are specifically instructed to do so. They are distinctly sensitive to the wishes of higher authority, and do not wish to risk offending it.

The survey noted in Chapter 5, conducted by Rosalind Barnett and Professor Renato Tagiuri, of the Harvard Business School, indicates that of the young people aged seventeen and below contacted through subscribers to the *Harvard Business Review*, the females are much less likely to be considering managerial careers than the males. In response to the direct question, "Would you like to be a manager?" there were positive responses from 53 percent of the males and 35 percent of the females. But when various alternatives were presented and the question asked for the *most* preferred choices, 40 percent of the males and only 10 percent of the females chose management or business alternatives.

The picture which emerges is that a great many young women continue to reject management and business careers as unsuitable, and that this is why there are so few females in the professional schools that prepare people for occupations in business. Studies conducted by Virginia Schein, of Metropolitan Life Insurance Company, indicate that managing is viewed as largely a masculine occupation. Successful middle managers are considered to possess characteristics, attitudes, and temperaments of a kind more commonly ascribed to men than to

EXHIBIT 30
Motivation to Manage of Male and Female Business Administration Majors

Motivation to Manage	Male Students	Female Students
High Motivation	346 (51%)	25 (39%)
Low Motivation	328 (49%)	39 (61%)
Favorable Attitude Toward Authority		
High Motivation	295 (44%)	37 (58%)
Low Motivation	379 (56%)	27 (42%)
Desire to Compete		
High Motivation	376 (56%)	28 (44%)
Low Motivation	298 (44%)	36 (56%)
Assertive Motivation		
High Motivation	207 (31%)	11 (17%)
Low Motivation	467 (69%)	53 (83%)
Desire to Exercise Power		
High Motivation	355 (53%)	21 (33%)
Low Motivation	319 (47%)	43 (67%)
Desire for a Distinctive Position		
High Motivation	473 (70%)	43 (67%)
Low Motivation	201 (30%)	21 (33%)
Sense of Responsibility		
High Motivation	339 (50%)	35 (55%)
Low Motivation	335 (50%)	29 (45%)

women. To the extent that women accept this view, and many clearly do, they simply will not flock into managerial work in large numbers. Presumably the lesser managerial motivation of college women is a factor in this decision.

Based on what is known now it appears that a high proportion of the women with a desire to manage have already found their way into management occupations. Such women certainly should be encouraged to follow managerial careers; they have a good prospect of succeeding. But fewer female college students than males want to manage, and, in spite of women's liberation, many females are not attracted to what they perceive as the masculine occupation of managing. To the extent that men also view the occupation as masculine they will tend to "discriminate" against women who may desire to become managers. All in all it becomes clear that if women are to be a major source of managerial talent, major cultural changes must occur, well beyond those that have already occurred, so that more women develop the motivation to manage and more men view the managerial role as appropriate for women.

This will require something more than the basic input strategy of selecting women with high intelligence, motivation to manage, and the requisite knowledge. Such a strategy at the present time will not come close to filling the needs of the management talent shortage. On the other hand, extension of the basic input strategy into more specific placements and the use of certain of the mediator strategies may yield more favorable results.

At this point I feel that the well-reasoned recommendations advanced by Professor Marshall Brenner, of the University of Southern California, offer the best guidelines for supplementing an initial effort to find and select female managers with true management potential. He makes the following suggestions:

1. Select and/or develop women who have expertise in

their field clearly superior to that of the great majority of the people to be supervised.

2. Explain to women candidates for management the organization's role requirements for a manager, and let them consider these requirements carefully before beginning development activity.
3. Select potential managerial positions for development and placement in areas where the occupations are least sex-typed.
4. Select positions where the majority of the subordinate personnel are experienced.
5. Select positions where the superior is exceptionally supportive for development and initial placement.
6. Select positions where expertise is a large and important component of authority.
7. Make role training a basic and continuing segment of management development.
8. Provide husbands of the development candidates with an understanding of the support functions required of them.
9. Establish interacting groups of eight to twelve management development candidates, both male and female, and maintain the consistency of these groups.
10. Provide visibility for a program of "womanagement" development.

At the present time women can provide only a partial solution to the need for effective executive talent. In the future, assuming a continuation of current societal trends and appropriate company action, their contribution can be much greater. The crucial need is to overcome a major deficiency in the will to manage in a society where this motive is already in decline.

Minority Groups as a Source of Managerial Talent

While minority-group members, primarily blacks, represent

roughly 11 percent of the total labor force, they hold only slightly over 3 percent of the managerial positions. This latter figure is up from the 2.5 percent existing in 1960, but the upward trend has not been of sufficient magnitude to affect the fact that the great majority of minority-group members do not work as managers; they are distinctly overrepresented in the lower level occupations.

A Bureau of National Affairs, Inc., survey conducted in 1971 indicates that minorities are much more likely to be in management in the larger companies and at the lower levels. Of the organizations studied, 45 percent had no minorities in middle management at all, and 67 percent had none in top management. The failure to utilize blacks and other minority-group members in management is most pronounced in the manufacturing sector. The BNA survey indicates an increase in the number of minority-group members in management positions over the preceding five years, with the most pronounced changes occurring in the larger firms. The major reported obstacle to more extensive use of minorities in management was a lack of qualifications, although discrimination, prejudice, and stereotyping were mentioned as affecting promotion in some companies.

Clearly discrimination may be an aspect of company policy, although because of existing legislation this is likely to be true only in an informal, unofficial sense. In such cases the minority groups offer no possibility of providing a solution to executive talent shortages as long as the discrimination continues. On the other hand, among companies that are willing to use minority-group members more widely in management, the question of the amount of managerial potential existing there does become relevant.

To date, my efforts to study motivation to manage among blacks have been relatively unrewarding; thus I do not have the same kind of information on success relationships and motivation levels for minorities that I have for women. The business school groups contain practically no minority-group members, and although the liberal arts student sample does include a few blacks, the number is insufficient to allow conclusions to be drawn. In one study of first-line supervisors in a large manufacturing firm we have found that the black males have a higher motivation to manage than the whites, male or female. This finding is encouraging and is consistent with the fact that the personnel managers responding to the BNA survey did not view lack of motivation as a major obstacle to minority-group members assuming positions in management.

In contrast, however, lack of requisite qualifications and education was viewed as a major obstacle, in fact *the* major obstacle, to minority-group members becoming managers. The very small number of blacks in university business and engineering curricula supports this observation. It is apparent that minority groups have not been attracted to professional schools which inculcate the knowledge needed to manage effectively. This situation may be undergoing some change in certain quarters. The graduate business schools at Harvard, Columbia, and the University of Chicago are actively seeking black students and have had some success in these efforts. Atlanta University has conducted a master's-level program primarily for blacks for some years. There are other signs of change in some of the major state universities. But it remains true that the number of minority-group members with a solid knowledge base in the areas needed for effective functioning in business management is disproportionately low at the present time.

This problem is compounded, and probably in part caused, by the fact that blacks in the United States currently average well below the population as a whole in intelligence, as measured by conventional tests. Many writers have commented on this fact and a variety of explanations have been offered. It is sufficient to note here with Professor Abraham Korman, of the City University of New York, that insofar as employment is concerned, "The evidence is consistent and overwhelming that the predominant features of the black American are a generally lower level of verbal and symbolic achievement and a more negative self-image." Professor Korman adds, ". . . those companies which are seeking to meaningfully implement changes in the job status of the black American will have to develop methods and procedures which recognize these problems and which attempt to deal with them."

Given the small number of black managers and what is known about the range and distribution of measured intelligence among blacks, it is evident that a pool of unused intellectual talent does exist in the minority population. However, it is not likely to be of sufficient size to offer a major solution to problems of managerial talent shortages, especially when the deficit in relevant knowledge is considered as well.

What I have said should not be interpreted as indicating in any way that I oppose moving minority group members who possess managerial potential into management positions. In fact I favor such action very strongly for a number of reasons, including eliminating the effects of past discrimination and dealing effectively with governmental pressures regarding fair employment practices. On the other hand, these governmental pressures have already caused many firms to engage in extensive searches for management potential among the minorities, and while more extensive searches may unearth even more talent, the amount of minority talent which is so to speak "ready to go" insofar as managing is concerned simply is nowhere near enough to fill the impending need at the present time.

Again, as with women, the basic input strategy alone does not appear adequate to the task. Such a strategy must at the very least be supplemented with mediator strategies which emphasize knowledge training and occupational adjustment. There is evidence, for instance, that blacks perform much more effectively when they are competing with other blacks than when they are placed in competition with whites, presumably because of deficiencies in self-esteem relative to whites. Findings such as this provide guidance as to how black managers might best be utilized. But even with such knowledge it is apparent that sizable increases in the number of effectively functioning minority-group managers will occur only over a considerable period of time.

Internal Search for Management Potential

The upgrading programs that have been instituted by a number of companies tend to stress identification and development of management potential among women and minorities, largely because that is where the governmental pressure is strongest. Yet such programs can be extended to include all types of employees. Thus a company might seek out management potential in employee groups which previously have been tapped only rarely as a source of managers, and then only for promotions to the first level. In most cases these will be people who lack a college education. Among males a college degree typically has meant automatic qualification, at least as a candidate, for managerial work.

How useful might this previously untapped, less well-educated group be as a major source of managerial talent? Although the internal-search strategy has much to recommend it and certainly may unearth some outstanding managers, I feel it would be overly optimistic to view it as a long-term solution to managerial shortages.

At least in the managerial groups I have studied, motivation to manage does not appear to be any lower among those who have not attended college than among those who have. Whether the same is true at lower occupational levels I do not know; also, I do not have specific data bearing on the question of whether motivation to manage has been declining in the noncollege population as it has among college students On the latter question, however, there is sufficient related information to make it almost certain that some decline has occurred in all major segments of our society.

Even with the uncertainty regarding the available level of managerial motivation, other considerations raise serious questions regarding the ultimate usefulness of the internal-search strategy without the addition of mediators such as training and job restructuring. Higher education does provide knowledge needed to manage increasingly complex business operations, and the institutions of higher learning now do attract a high proportion of those with the intelligence required for much managerial work. Thus the noncollege population would appear to be relatively deficient in relevant knowledge and intelligence, even if it is not in motivation to manage. Knowledge of the kind required for first-level supervision may not be as much of a problem, but at higher levels and in many staff positions this is not true. Furthermore, as higher and higher proportions of each successive age group go to college, the remaining pool of superior intelligence in the noncollege population inevitably will shrink. Thus, a strategy that in years past might have been highly rewarding offers much less promise today.

This is not to say that internal search cannot yield some payoff in managerial talent, only that it has certain inherent drawbacks, at least in the short term. One approach is to advertise within the company workforce asking employees to notify the personnel department if they wish to be considered for promotion to management. Those who indicate interest can be evaluated in terms of their knowledge, intelligence, and motivation to manage using psychological measuring instruments and other similar procedures. Those who exhibit management potential can then be placed in a reserve talent pool while continuing in their regular jobs until selected for actual promotion. A variant of this approach involves widescale application of psychological measures. Candidates for more refined screening are then identified on the basis of these test scores rather than through a voluntary bidding process. Talent searches of this kind may, of course, be equally, if not even more, applicable in the upgrading of women and minorities.

The Input Strategies Overall

In addition to women, minorities, and the noncollege population, there are several other sources of managerial talent that might be considered. Among these are college graduates in fields other than business and engineering, and foreign nationals.

The discussion in Chapter 4 brought out the fact that liberal arts majors tend to be particularly low in motivation to manage, and in addition, most will have little knowledge of business matters. This, then, appears to be a managerial talent source which, although extremely valuable in the past, now is well on its way to drying up. Students in professional programs other than business show managerial motivation which more nearly approximates that of business majors, but with the exception of those in engineering and journalism, few are likely to gravitate to business management.

Foreign nationals might well provide a potential solution, especially for companies which operate multinationally. In terms of relevant knowledge and intelligence there is certainly a sizable talent pool to draw on. Studies of motivation to manage have not yet extended into the international arena to any meaningful degree, but there is no reason to believe that there are not enough highly motivated individuals somewhere in the rest of the world to fill the need. The major problems here have nothing to do with deficiencies in aspects of management potential. Rather they relate to the willingness of American firms to follow this route on a truly extensive basis, and the willingness of highly qualified foreign nationals to join American firms in this country on a major scale.

Given the current state of national loyalities I seriously doubt that either of these things will happen. American firms doing business around the world will certainly make some use of managers from other countries here. In fact there are currently a number of such individuals holding top-level jobs in major American corporations. But to take this course frequently enough to fill the gap between managerial supply and demand is another matter. To my knowledge no society in history has consistently given its higher paying and more prestigious jobs to members of another society. Furthermore, companies that do not operate outside this country are in a relatively weak position insofar as obtaining foreign nationals is concerned, and other countries can be expected ultimately to respond with countermeasures when they see their managerial talent being drained away.

Overall it appears that tapping new sources of talent can be of considerable help, but that no one source is likely to provide the needed management potential alone. Furthermore, many of the new sources exhibit marked deficiencies in one respect or another. In practically every case there is a clear need for some type of development effort which goes beyond simply hiring a person as a management candidate. There is very little management potential lying around "ready to go"; however, there is a certain amount of raw material available in these new talent sources, which might ultimately be turned into management potential.

10

The Computer as Manager

If a company cannot solve its staffing problems through recruiting, selection, and resorting to new talent sources, what can it do? The answer is clear — it can change. Either the organization itself can change in some way so as to adapt to its people, or it can change its people to adapt to the organization.

A useful approach to studying change has been developed by Professor Harold Leavitt, of Stanford University. In his view, change may be achieved in one of three ways — using technological, structural, or "people" approaches. In essence Professor Leavitt is talking about three broad categories of mediator processes that can intervene and have an influence on performance output. Strategies may be developed which place primary emphasis on technological change, on structural change, or on people change as a method of dealing with managerial talent shortages.

The technological approach to solving human resource problems typically has taken the form of replacing people with machines. Frequently companies have dealt with skill shortages, labor conflict, high wage costs, and the like, by introducing more advanced, automated equipment which requires fewer people to operate. In the case of managerial talent shortages, this approach would suggest reducing the need for managers by utilizing computers extensively in the decision-making process; in effect, managers would be replaced by computers.

The structural approach is essentially that of organization planning. The work and the organization are redesigned to make them more compatible with the people. In days past, when the American labor force contained large numbers of immigrants who lacked industrial skills, companies resorted to extensive division of labor and work simplification in order to minimize the need for learning; now with a very different type of labor force we see a move to job enlargement and job enrichment. With reference to managerial talent shortages, the structural approach would call for a change to a more participative or power-equalized type of organization. Low motivation to manage would be accepted as inevitable, hierarchy would be largely abolished, and something approaching the participatory democracy of the campus activists would be installed.

A technological approach accepts the organization and the type of people it needs as given, and then changes the technology. A structural approach views the technology and the type of people available as constants, and then changes the way the work is organized. In contrast, *the people approach* emphasizes changing people while leaving technology and structure largely as is, at least initially. Historically the people approach has been utilized relatively infrequently in American industry, although it is inherent in a certain amount of what has been done in the name of management and organization development. As a solution to management talent shortages it would involve changing people to give them a greater will to manage.

In this chapter I will consider the technological approach. Ensuing chapters will deal with the structural and people approaches.

The Expected Demise of Middle Management

In 1958 Professor Leavitt, along with Professor Thomas Whisler, of the University of Chicago, wrote an article predicting that the new technology compounded out of computers and mathematical decision-making tools would rapidly displace middle management. Their expectation was that the need for policymaking at the top and supervision at the bottom would make upper and lower level managements relatively resistant to the inroads of the computer, but that middle management would prove expendable. This viewpoint continues to be given considerable credence today, as evidenced by a recent article by Robert Hicks, of the Army and Air Force Exchange Service. It is an attractive idea in the context of management talent shortages because it implies a decreased demand for managers, as computers increasingly provide most of the information flow to top management that middle management previously provided.

The argument is that as qualified managers become scarcer, companies should invest more heavily in computers and rely more heavily on the decision-making aids of management science and operations research. In doing this these companies should find less need for managers, especially at the middle level. Whether the reduction achieved would be of a magnitude sufficient to alleviate the shortage fully is an open question, but at the very least it should make a sizable contribution to that end.

To evaluate the approach of solving talent needs through technological investment and change, it is necessary to study situations where computers have been introduced. Does the number of managers decline under these circumstances, or does the anticipated technological displacement fail to occur?

Studies conducted to date indicate that when computers are introduced into the corporate environment the major effects on personnel are at the clerical level, where reductions in the number of people required for routine work tend to be sizable. If a reduction in personnel occurs at the managerial level, however, it is much less pronounced. Usually there is no decline in the number of managers, and if there is it is not nearly as great as the decline in clerical workers; thus the *ratio* of managers never declines.

Research conducted in a shoe company by Professor Hak Chong Lee, of the University of New York at Albany, yields a typical result. With the advent of the computer, line clerical departments decreased in size, although the managerial decrease was minimal. But the data processing units increased, particularly at the managerial level. The net effect was an increase of roughly 20 percent in managers and a comparable decrease in clerical personnel. Results such as these offer little basis for hope that technological change and expanded use of computers will provide a solution to managerial talent shortages. Furthermore, managerial jobs often appear to be expanded and to become more complex after a computer is introduced. Thus, the need for highly competent managers, who can manage people and machines in interaction, may well be even greater.

Why Is Middle Management Needed?

In his book *New Power for Mangement: Computer Systems and Management Science*, David Hertz, of McKinsey & Company, makes the point that the new technology, rather than displacing management, upgrades its decisions. "The major impact of management science . . . has been to force management to face new kinds of decisions on a new level of decision making with new forms of information." Elsewhere he notes that "decision making moves to a new and perhaps more difficult level." With considerable experience in assisting in the installation of computer-based decision systems, Dr. Hertz qualifies as a highly competent observer of the current scene.

Research conducted by Professors Vaughn Blankenship, of the State University of New York at Buffalo, and Raymond Miles, of the University of California at Berkeley, provides further insight. They found, in a study of decision making among 190 managers in 8 companies, that although the top-level managers tended to make the final choice, to have the greatest perceived influence, to be most free from superiors, and to rely to the greatest extent on subordinates, they did not initiate the most decisions. This role fell primarily to middle management, although in the smaller firms lower level managers were frequently involved as well. These data do not fit with the view that decisions are solely a matter for the upper levels of mangement, with implementation and supervision the major concern below. Levels below the top emerge as an integral part of the decision-making process, serving to identify problems, recommend actions, initiate deliberations, and develop innovative, perhaps even creative, proposals.

What appears to be happening is that the introduction of new technology does in fact influence middle management jobs — not to obliterate them, but to raise the level of sophistication and the complexity of the decision-initiation process. With more information and better mathematical tools, middle managers are able to see new problems and identify more alternative solutions. It is clear that these jobs now require even higher levels of relevant knowledge and intelligence than they did previously. They may also require more will to manage, although this is not as self-evident. In any event, there is no basis for hypothesizing a decline in managerial motivation requirements.

Impact of Technology on Structure

If the introduction of a computer-based technology does not offer much hope of directly alleviating managerial talent shortages, what effect does it have? The resulting changes might, for instance, serve to condition the effects of structural and people approaches to the problem. What is the impact of the new technology on the way organizations function and the way people behave?

A considerable amount of information is accumulating regarding the impact of computer systems on organizational structure. The more comprehensive studies have indicated repeatedly that there is a tendency for at least some types of decisions to move upward to higher levels in the organizational hierarchy, and for a greater amount of control to be exercised from the top down. A primary factor in this increased centralization appears to be the availability of information at higher levels which the computer makes possible.

When computers are used merely to perform routine computational tasks, as often happens, rather than to provide information for decision making, little centralization seems to occur. This is true of many applications in the accounting area, such as billing and payroll. Furthermore, centralization following the introduction of computers, even for decision-making purposes, does not immediately and inevitably result in centralization of decisions in all areas involved.

Higher level management can use the computer to obtain data that would not otherwise be available. These data can become available at corporate headquarters with a minimal time lag, so that decisions based on them can be made just as if a top-level manager were physically present at the point where the information originates. Thus those at the top may choose to make many decisions, and in fact typically do so. But the same information can be made available at lower levels as well. There is nothing about computer systems that requires a flow of information only to the top. There are instances in which upper management simply does not have the time to make all the decisions it theoretically could given the new fund of information provided by a computer. Thus, some types of decision making may in fact be decentralized as a result of computerization.

Yet even when decentralization does occur in the context of computers, the computer permits and typically produces a considerable exercise of control from the top. Without computers, this control of decentralized operations is obtained via budgeting and managerial accounting systems, procedures that tend to permit long periods when a manager can act at his own discretion before controls are activated. With computers, monitoring of lower level decisions and their effects can be practically continuous. Thus, although the locus for certain kinds of decisions can be, and often is, moved downward, the computer introduces a capability not available previously for intervention by top management, should these decisions stray too far from established policy.

The degree to which centralization actually does occur with the advent of the computer appears to vary from one area of the business to another. Data processing and logistics tend to become much more centralized. The same is true of manufacturing. But a similar degree of centralization does not usually appear in the marketing component. At least in the long term, computers provide the flexibility required so that decisions can be made by the individuals most qualified to make them, while upgrading the quality of the decisions themselves by providing more, and more valid, data. In many cases the result is centralization.

One of the most comprehensive analyses in this area was carried out by Professor Whisler in twenty-three life insurance companies. He found that computers not only contributed to greater centralization, but that they often had diametrically opposite effects on the clerical workers and on their immediate supervisors. Although in both groups a sizable proportion of jobs remained unchanged, when change did occur for the supervisors it was usually toward an enlarged and more complex job. Among the clerical workers, on the other hand, the reverse was true; a majority of them experienced job routinization and diminished requirements. When Professor Whisler's data are combined with those from other studies, it becomes clear that the overall trend with computerization is for managerial jobs to expand both in number and in the extent of responsibilities, with more positions being affected in this manner at each successive rung up the managerial ladder. Nonmanagerial jobs tend to become more routinized and simplified, although there is considerable variability of effect from job to job.

Another area of impact is found in the distribution of decision-making authority between staff and line. Generally there is a shift of authority away from the line and into staff units, especially those closely allied to data processing.

EXHIBIT 31

*The Effects of Computers on Clerical
and Supervisory Job Size in
Twenty-Three Insurance Companies*

Departments	Job Dimished	Job Enlarged	Job Unchanged
Supervisory Jobs			
New Business	14%	28%	58%
Policy Service	0	25%	75%
Accounting	4%	40%	56%
Actuarial	0	36%	64%
All Departments	4%	35%	61%
Clerical Jobs			
New Business	24%	24%	52%
Policy Service	14%	31%	55%
Accounting	39%	24%	37%
Actuarial	26%	15%	59%
All Departments	31%	22%	47%

As reported by Thomas L. Whisler in *The Impact of Computers on Organizations.*

In line with this staff emphasis is a tendency to move to a functional form of organization with separate marketing, production, accounting, personnel, and other departments. Geographical departmentalization tends to disappear, but the use of product lines as a basis for organizational grouping may disappear also.

Impact of Technology on People

In contrast to the impact of computers on structure, their impact on people has received minimal study. We know very little about how people are changed when computer systems are introduced. It is apparent, however, that among those who know little about computers and mathematical decision-making tools, there can be considerable negative feeling aroused; anxiety, resentment, and uncertainty can become widespread. This tends to be less true of younger managers, many of whom are quite knowledgeable in this area, and of top-level managers, who view themselves as in control and thus threatened very little.

Overall, it seems unlikely that computer systems will exercise any direct negative effect on the younger generation of managers coming up, who are likely to have been trained in the use of computers and in mathematical techniques in college, and are thus least likely to view computers as competitors. Furthermore, because they possess knowledge in this area which many manages who are older and superior to them in rank do not, they may well feel more self-confident and sure of themselves because the computer is there.

On the other hand, the indirect effects of technological advances mediated through structural changes do not appear as promising. Managerial jobs will become more demanding and complex at a time when the supply of people who want to manage is low. Computer systems will exert pressures toward centralization, even though younger managerial aspirants want decentralization and participatory democracy. The potential for close control from above will reach its highest level when those subject to this control are the most likely to be vehemently opposed to any restriction of their freedom by higher authority. Forces opposed to the formation of small, geographically segregated units will be introduced when the desire for such units should be at a maximum.

This is not to say that other factors related to expanded computer use may not mesh well with the known characteristics of the younger generation: A computerized technology requires relevant knowledge and intelligence, for instance, and places an emphasis on staff authority and professional expertise. But it remains true that many aspects of computer technology seem to be at odds with what we know of the country's youth. Furthermore, it can often have structural effects that differ sharply from those associated with participative management and organization development. I will return to this constraining effect of the new technology in subsequent chapters, when I consider these two techniques as possible solutions to managerial manpower shortages.

In any event, evidence from a variety of directions points to the conclusion that the new technology is unlikely to offer much aid in alleviating the crunch in executive talent. In fact, the new technology may actually accentuate the problem by limiting the effectiveness of certain alternative structural and people-based approaches.

11

The Participative Alternative

The battlecry of "participatory democracy" was heard frequently on college campuses during the late 1960s and early
1970s. Decisions that frequently involved some new attack on
university authority evolved out of group deliberations which
effectively prevented the attribution of responsibility for acts of
violence to specific individuals. Such commitment to group
rather than individual decision making and shared rather than
individual leadership fits well with the declining will to manage
in the student population.

Professor Herbert Wilcox, of New York University, notes
that "the widely publicized youth revolt has raised its banners
against hierarchy — and authority." He adds, "An ideological
counterpart to the remonstrances of the younger generation are
the fulmination and prophesies of organization theorists and
management consultants who see in the death of hierarchy the
liberation of humanity." Although Professor Wilcox is not sym-
pathetic to these forces, he sees them coalescing to produce
strong pressures on business and government to alter existing
structures so as to minimize the emphasis on hierarchic authority and maximize the use of participative alternatives. Many

other writers, such as Professor Gloria Cowan, of Wayne State University, alternately argue that business will "have to" and "should" adapt its structures to the new values of youth.

Given these pressures and the apparent attractiveness of utilizing a participative strategy to reduce the need for a motivation to manage which is dwindling, it becomes crucial to study what is known about participative management. Will such a structural-change approach work?

The Need for Control

There has been considerable misunderstanding as to what participative management is. It is *not* token consultation with those at lower levels for the purpose of obtaining greater compliance and more effective implementation of decisions already made. Nor is it abandonment of control in the firm so that people are left free to do what they please. What it *is* is a drastic shift in the locus of control. The term "power equalization" is often used to describe the downward flow of actual control over decisions which occurs when participative procedures are initiated.

Yet the use of the term power equalization may be misleading. When students talk about participatory democracy, they do not mean equalization of power from top to bottom, but rather a system which concentrates power over decisions, important and trivial, at the lowest level, in the hands of the majority. In my opinion no mere power equalization, which leaves upper organizational levels intact, if somewhat bereft of authority, will satisfy existing pressures and eliminate the need for the dissipating motivation to manage. It will take something much more drastic than that.

There is considerable evidence that simply eliminating or minimizing control over those who work for an organization so that each can "do his own thing" is no solution. The so-called *laissez-faire* leadership style, under which the nominal manager does not even participate in discussions other than to provide information if asked, and makes no effort to see that decisions are either made or carried out, has been studied. Although subordinates are not entirely unhappy with this approach, very little is accomplished. To the extent that organizations operate with low levels of control, they consistently have been found to be less effective.

The need for some kind of control has been clearly recognized by researchers from the University of Michigan's Institute for Social Research, where participative management ideology had its origins. Professors Donald Pelz and Frank Andrews report that even among scientists in research laboratories, high levels of freedom to do what they please are associated with reduced levels of scientist effectiveness. Professor Arnold Tannenbaum finds that organizations with very little control anywhere in the system tend to be ineffective. He also finds that although too much control at the top can be a source of difficulty, so, too, can too much at the bottom. Under circumstances where control is very unequally distributed at one level or another, there is a high risk that the needs of individuals will take precedence over the goals of the organization. Under such circumstances a company can in a very real sense be "plundered." The latter finding raises a serious question about introducing the deep levels of decentralization that many of the younger generation advocate.

Although most of us tend to think in terms of control exercised downward through a managerial hierarchy, there are in fact other ways in which the needed control can be obtained. These other methods are consistently favored by the ideologues of participative management. One such approach is to use the value system and ethical precepts of a profession. Professional codes clearly do control members of the professions, and may substitute for hierarchic authority in this regard. In medical or legal practice, and even in the faculty component of a university, this kind of control can be very effective, but in most companies it is inadequate — the number of professionals is too small.

Similarly, a sizable element of control may be exercised in certain jobs by the task itself and the pressure of the situation. The pace of the assembly line does control production workers to some extent, and the crush of customers often has a similar impact on sales clerks. Yet, again, this type of "task control" is not inherent in all jobs, and in many cases it does not work very well where it is present. As with professional control, the control exercised by the inherent nature of the work is unlikely to be adequate to the needs of most companies.

In contrast, however, coworkers, work groups, peers, and other formal and informal units are common to practically all organizations. These groups can exercise control over their members, and it is primarily this type of control with which participative management is concerned. The groups can reach decisions on a majority if not a consensus basis, and can exert pressure for universal conformity with these decisions. Thus there is control, and there can, of course, be a tyranny of the majority just as there can be tyranny by duly constituted authority.

A problem with this type of control is whether the group decision and the pressure to implement it are consonant with the goals of the organization. In a small company, the group and the organization are sufficiently congruent to produce many common objectives. In a large company, groups multiply and organizational distances are extended; consonance of goals becomes more of a problem. Under these circumstances there is a sizable risk that without the continuing influence of hierarchic authority (and thus a continuing need for motivation to manage), groups may go off on their own and seek their own ends, quite independent of corporate objectives.

The World of Practice

One key question involves the extent to which existing managements can be expected to embrace participative approaches.

If there is overwhelming opposition to them, then it cannot be considered a viable alternative for most firms, at least for the present. This does not mean that later solid evidence of proven effectiveness might not make participative management more attractive, however.

A number of surveys have been conducted to determine how managers feel about participative management. The upshot seems to be that although various activities that have become associated with participative management, such as counseling subordinates and developing effective communication, are viewed quite favorably, the core aspect involving a shift of control over decisions to lower levels is not so widely favored. Professor Rama Krishnan, of Youngstown State University in Ohio, finds relatively little support for such a shift of decision-making power among manufacturing company executives. He compares his data with those from a recent *Harvard Business Review* survey and finds somewhat more support for participative decisions in the latter. However, the Harvard sample contained many nonmanagers — professors, consultants, and the like — and these people were much more likely to favor participative approaches; so too were the respondents under thirty, as might be expected.

A number of companies report having adopted participative approaches to varying degrees. However, few of these cases appear to involve very drastic shifts in the type and level of control. A recent review of what is being done along these lines is presented by Professor Carroll Swart, of Ball State University. His report indicates that the tempo of activity on the participative front is picking up. Yet other experience makes it clear that companies may indulge in participative approaches when business is good and profits high only to revoke them when the pressure of business competition becomes more acute. The very fact that they can be revoked suggests that decision control never did move fully to the lower levels.

EXHIBIT 32
Degree of Support for Various
Uses of a Participative Approach

Question	Degree of Agreement	
	Managers in Manufacturing Firms in the Midwest	*Harvard Business Review* Readers
If your company were considering moving one of its offices or plants to another location, do you think the employees in the offices or plants should be asked to vote on the sites being considered by management?	19%	36%
Suppose your company's policy toward hiring members of minority groups became controversial for some reason. Do you think employees should then be entitled to vote on the hiring policy or policies which they would most like to see followed?	9%	15%
Directors should never select a new chief executive of a company without accurate knowledge first of his acceptability to key managerial or other employee groups.	10%	12%

Adapted from an article by Rama Krishnan in the June 1974 issue of *Academy of Management Journal.*

There are a number of reasons why only a relatively small number of managers appear ready to embrace participative management fully at the present time. One is that the approach is closely identified both conceptually and historically with the human relations movement of an earlier period, and much of the skepticism generated by that movement has been transferred to its offspring. Furthermore, the close relationship between participation and socialist ideology has apparently not gone unnoticed. Although for many of its advocates this association makes participative management uniquely attractive, a reverse reaction can be expected from the current generation of American managers.

Then, too, there still are many first-rate managers who possess high levels of motivation to manage. What is to be done with them, with all their experience and knowledge of business operations? Under a fully participative system they would have to undergo drastic motivational changes or leave. Very few companies are willing to risk throwing away their existing, seasoned executive talent in this manner, and very few top-level executives are willing to do this to themselves.

How Good Is Participation?

Much early research on the subject of participative management utilized measures of the degree to which subordinates felt they were involved in decision making or viewed their superior as participative, and compared these with indexes of job satisfaction or productivity measured at the same time. This is an appropriate research strategy, because if nothing meaningful were to emerge from such studies, the participative approach could be rejected without the further effort of conducting the much more difficult research needed to establish causation. In general these so-called correlational studies have been successful; participation has proved to be related positively to job satisfaction almost without exception, and to be related to productivity often enough to require further study.

In addition to this type of research there was, even in the early period, some effort to determine whether participation *caused* satisfaction and high productivity. Such studies involved introducing participative techniques and then observing outcomes over time. Many of the early studies of this kind were conducted in the plants of the Harwood Manufacturing Company. Although this research was not well controlled, in that the results may well have been a consequence of factors other than participation per se, positive findings did emerge, and these were interpreted at the time as demonstrating the value of the participative approach.

More recent experimental studies of the kind that permit attribution of cause have been less favorable. Clearly, participation does cause higher morale and satisfaction at work, and a happier group of employees. But it does not have the same impact on performance. Many of the studies show no significant change in productivity as a consequence of participative management, while a number find an actual decrease. Thus, a study by Professor Reed Powell and John Schlacter, of Ohio State University, showed little evidence of productivity change with lesser degrees of participation, but when the group assumed the entire responsibility for work scheduling, performance fell off badly.

The current picture of participative management is distinctly unfavorable if one is concerned with such matters as productivity, output, and performance. On the other hand, the technique may be useful in solving morale problems. By sharing even a small amount of its authority, management often can obtain some alleviation of dissatisfactions.

Sources of Misinterpretation

A question remains as to why the correlational studies and the early field experiments produced the results they did. Why was there such enthusiasm for the participative approach?

One line of explanation takes the position that the results were obtained not because of the participation involved, but because of other factors that in these studies often went along with the participative approach. Among these *other factors,* all of which are known to have the potential for improving performance, are:

1. The setting of definite production goals by those involved in the participative decision making.

2. The existence of a considerable degree of higher level management support for the particular decisions reached on a participative basis, and the full knowledge of this support among those involved.

3. The greater degree of job knowledge accruing to the participative decision makers as a result of the lengthy discussions which preceded the decisions.

4. The existence of incentive payment systems which rewarded productivity and which paralleled the participation.

Most of these factors are of a kind which could explain the results of certain studies, but not of others. Probably the most pervasive is the goal-setting feature. Professors Stephen Carroll, of the University of Maryland, and Henry Tosi, of Michigan State University, have shown that one of the most crucial factors accounting for the success of a management-by-objectives program is the extent to which clear and relevant goals are in fact established. In contrast, the degree to which the subordinate rather than the superior influences these goals, and thus the degree of participation involved, is unrelated to the effectiveness of MBO. Since the goal-setting factor was not taken into account in a number of the early studies on participative management, it is entirely possible that what was demonstrated was the value of goal-setting, not of participation.

Another source of difficulty applies only to the so-called correlational research, where measures of the degree of participation and of effectiveness are taken at the same time. At first when positive relationships were found in such studies it was taken as self-evident that participative management *caused* superior performance, but later findings make it clear that this conclusion is not warranted.

There is conclusive evidence that outstanding performance is much more likely to produce leader behavior that falls in the participative category than that participation will cause outstanding performance. In these studies the performance of subordinates was varied and managerial behavior then observed. Professors Aaron Lowin, of Iowa State University, and James Craig, of Western Kentucky University, find that poor performers tend to elicit very close supervision with frequent directions and checking. The ideas of the subordinate are ignored, and he is held closely to prescribed procedures. Generally the poor performers are viewed as irresponsible, and treated with a minimum of kindness; they elicit anything but participative management. Professors Barry Goodstadt and David Kipnis, of Temple University, have conducted studies indicating that when the poor performance is associated with attitude problems and a lack of cooperation, supervisors tend to become exceedingly coercive. It is apparent that when there is a close association between participation and effective performance, it is often true that the very fact of having effective subordinates accounts for the greater consideration and respect given to the opinions of subordinates. In effect, the performance *causes* the participation. Furthermore, the participative situation can be expected to continue only as long as things are going well; when the situation becomes tight and crises are on the horizon, there is a marked tendency to revert to more authoritarian and hierarchic modes of supervision. The implication is that only the very successful companies can afford to become highly participative, and then only as long as they remain successful.

The Quality of Participative Decisions

Another question involves the quality of the decisions that come out of the participative process. Are they better or worse than what one might expect of a competent manager making decisions unilaterally.

It is evident from research that more and better ideas emerge when a number of individuals work on a problem alone than when these same individuals work on the problem together, as in the typical participative group. This finding was originally obtained with students, but it has now been confirmed with employed groups, including research scientists, advertising men, and managers. Working in a group often has an inhibitory effect on the generation of ideas which is not present when people work alone.

This cannot be interpreted as meaning that decisions are best made by a single manager working in isolation. The inclusion of a number of people in the decision-making process brings new knowledge, viewpoints, and insights to bear. Most groups do a better job of decision making than do most single individuals, given a comparable level of relevant knowledge, although the groups tend to take considerably longer to reach their decisions and under certain circumstances are more likely to take high risks.

The problem is, however, that in most business situations the higher level manager often is more experienced, better informed, more knowledgeable, and better educated than the lower level subordinates. He has the power of expertise, and this power may be even more in evidence in the future, as the bounds of knowledge are extended. Studies conducted at Utrecht University, in the Netherlands, by Professors Mauk Mulder and Henk Wilke indicate that where there is such a difference in expertise within a group, the very existence of the participative group context tends to enhance the power of the expert. His opinions are accepted uncritically and alternative proposals are not advanced. Thus, the advantages of multiple inputs to the decision are lost; the participative situation when there is a sizable knowledge differential has much the same result as the isolated manager making decisions without consultation.

Thus, unless groups are composed of individuals who have essentially the same perceived capacity to contribute to a decision, participation can be expected to yield decisions of lower quality than those emerging out of current practices, which usually involve widespread consultation, staff work, and the like. Those involved in the participative process may well be more motivated to implement the decisions, due to a sense of personal involvement, public commitment, and group pressure, but at the same time this motivation may lead them down a road which is in fact not the best one. Since differences in expertise are characteristic in most business situations, it may be difficult to find cases where participation does not do more harm than good, because it short-circuits the normal practice of conferring with a number of individuals who work independently.

Pressures for Centralization

The participative alternative as a structural-change strategy cannot be evaluated in terms of its potential for solving the managerial talent shortage problem only. Even if it should appear very attractive for dealing with talent shortages, it might have to be rejected because of negative side effects or because it is opposed by other considerations. There are, in fact, two pressures operating in American society at the present time, which can be expected to increase in importance in the future, and which diminish the attractiveness of participative management.

One of these, the pressure for centralization, was discussed in the preceding chapter. Expanding computer technology at the very least offers increased opportunity for centralized decision making and control. When one studies actual situations where computers have been introduced for more than the purpose of performing routine tasks, it becomes apparent that the opportunity to centralize decisions typically is seized when it becomes available. The rational decision-making tools of operations research and management science, when added to a computer system, bring with them very explicit assumptions favoring centralized decision processes. It may be possible to have both participative management and the new technology, but the two constitute an unlikely combination. It is the very nature of the technology to emphasize individual expertise, rationality above all else, and hierarchic control via management-information systems. All of these pose serious problems for the participative approach.

Equally strong pressures for centralization arise out of what Eleanore Carruth, writing in *Fortune,* calls the "legal explosion." The number of lawsuits against companies has been escalating at an almost unbelievable rate. Those in the areas of environmental issues and fair employment practices represent relatively new developments, but older areas such as antitrust, securities regulation, and labor law are booming too. The number of suits filed in federal district courts in 1972 was almost 40 percent higher than for 1970 in the major areas of business activity.

The result has been a sizable increase in corporate legal staffs and in outlays for legal expenses. The advent of class-action suits in meaningful numbers has posed a particular threat. The highest settlement in such a suit to date totaled $117 million, in a case against five drug companies involving the pricing of the antibiotic tetracycline. However, the major source of legal problems remains the federal government, with state and local governments not far behind.

In a recent consent settlement of an action brought by the federal Equal Employment Opportunity Commission before the Federal Communications Commission, AT&T agreed to compensate women and minority employees with payments estimated to run between $12 and $15 million. The payments are intended as retroactive compensation to those who in the past may have been victims of discrimination in promotions, transfers, and salary administration. In addition, AT&T agreed to undertake a variety of steps aimed at achieving a balance between the proportions of women and minorities in its various occupations and the proportions existing in surrounding labor-force areas. The result of this agreement has been a considerable circumscribing of management's discretion in personnel matters.

EXHIBIT 33
Number of Lawsuits Filed in
Federal District Court by Area

Area in Which Lawsuits Filed	Year of First Available Data	Percent Increase in Number of Lawsuit in 1972
Environmental Issues	1968	538%
Fair Employment Practices	1972	*
Antitrust	1961	228%
Securities Regulation	1961	618%
Patents, Copyrights, and Trademarks	1961	38%
Labor Law	1961	101%

*Although a meaningful percent increase cannot be computed due to the lack of earlier data, the number of fair-employment-practices suits in 1972 was substantial, amounting to 9 percent of the total.

Adapted from data provided in an article by Eleanore Carruth in the April 1973 issue of *Fortune.*

In these cases the legal actions typically treat the corporation as a single entity and hold it responsible as a whole. The result is a strong pressure from the top for increased control over lower organizational levels and dispersed locations. Top management cannot afford to provide a high degree of freedom down the line; the risk that somebody will do something that will cost the company millions of dollars in legal judgments and fees is too great. The perhaps unintended result of the legal explosion is a strong pressure for centralization of decision making and intensification of controls. This consideration, in conjunction with the impact of the new computer-based technology, will inevitably serve to dampen enthusiasm for a decentralized, particpative approach in many companies.

Participation as a Strategy

There is reason to believe that some people want participation more than others and that the current younger generation contains large numbers of potential managers who desire and are ideologically committed to participatory democracy. Yet the approach appears to offer little advantage in terms of organizational effectiveness, and in its more extreme forms can be detrimental. Furthermore, there are strong counterpressures which directly oppose yielding to the desire for greater participation among the young.

Given these considerations, a companywide shift to the participative alternative hardly recommends itself as a solution to executive talent shortages occasioned by lessening motivation to manage. In all probability, a shift along these lines will bring with it a reduction in the need for a will to manage, to the extent that group control is substituted for hierarchic control. However, there are probable side effects of a comprehensive shift of this kind, in terms of reduced concern for organizational goals, inability to deal with crises, potential for corporate anarchy, vulnerability to legal action, failure to utilize the new technology effectively, wasted executive talent, and reduced profit performance. These side effects argue strongly against adopting this strategy on anything but a partial basis in business organizations of any size.

It is even possible that the participative approach is truly incapable of adoption wherever sizable differences in expertise exist, as they often do in business firms. Under such circumstances, the expected result would be either reinforcement of the power of current management or, alternatively, the rise to power of a new expert elite from among the "participating" younger members of the organization. Differences in expertise are minimal among the young, among students on campuses, for instance, and it may therefore be easy for youth groups to maintain a stable participatory state that is much more difficult to achieve as differences in experience, learning, and education develop with age.

Although I do not believe participative management offers an acceptable comprehensive solution to the management talent problem, there do appear to be times and circumstances where some movement in a participatory direction may prove desirable. Many people do like participation and become more satisfied with their work situation under such a system. Accordingly, a shift toward participative forms may be called for should the demands for a voice in decision making among the younger members in a particular part of an organization become so intense that a serious threat arises. Participation is unlikely to provide an answer to productivity problems, but it certainly can help in reducing conflict, restoring cooperation, and preventing needed employees from leaving in angry frustration.

When this kind of substitution of group for hierarchic control is made, it should be limited to what the demands of the particular situation require. In my opinion, participation is something management should accept only to the degree that it offers a practical solution to a business problem. It should not be instituted across the board when there is no likely benefit from it, merely because of an ideological commitment to greater democracy in organizational life.

In addition to its use in dealing with internal pressures, there is the prospect that the participative approach can be substituted for hierarchic control, and thus for motivation to manage, under certain circumstances without yielding serious negative consequences. In conjunction with other structural changes, and used with appropriate forethought and discretion, the participative alternative does appear to offer some potential for reducing the amount of managerial motivation needed. It cannot realistically be viewed as eliminating the need, because it is neither possible nor desirable totally to replace hierarchic with group control. However, it can be used in certain segments of a company, and thus serve to reduce the need. I will consider these uses along with other structural-change strategies in the next two chapters.

12

Organization Development

Organization development, or OD, is a much more recent addition to the business scene than the participative-management approach discussed in the last chapter. Yet in its brief life OD has enfolded the participative approach and moved to the forefront as the major strategy advocated by those who espouse humanism in organizations. It has been proposed as a panacea for almost every type of business ill, and has spawned a host of books and articles dealing with its applications. In a number of respects, including its rapid spread and its tendency to generate controversy, the organization development movement is not unlike the scientific management movement of an earlier era. Like scientific management, OD seems to espouse a "one best way." However, in other respects the two movements clearly are worlds apart. Their underlying values and goals are almost directly antithetical.

Given the rapid spread of organization development and its strong ideological and historical ties to participative management, the possibility of applying this approach to the solution of problems created by managerial talent shortages must be considered. In fact, writers such as Professors Frank Friedlander and

L. Dave Brown, of Case Western Reserve University, already have presented an argument for organization development based on its relationship to changing societal values and attitudes. It is true that much of what was said in Chapter 11 about participative management applies equally to organization development; in a number of respects my conclusions regarding the two are the same. Yet organization development goes well beyond mere participation and accordingly introduces certain new considerations that were not treated previously.

What Is Organization Development?

There is a great deal of confusion these days as to exactly what organization development is. The approach tends to be elusive and hard to pin down. In part this is because its practitioners and advocates have attempted to tie it to almost every positive value in American society, including political democracy and the Christian ethic. In part, also, it is because the OD approach is evolving on the basis of experience as it is used, and practitioners are constantly experimenting with new forms. Techniques which are consistent with the humanistic character of organization development tend to be incorporated into it almost as soon as they appear. Furthermore, the movement has created a new vocabulary which makes understanding difficult for those who have not yet learned the language.

The total OD process typically extends over a number of years, during which organization members move through a series of phases. The sequence proposed by Robert Blake and Jane Mouton, of Scientific Methods, Inc., an organization development consulting firm, is as follows:

Phase 1. Participants study the theory of managerial effectiveness underlying the approach and engage in T-group or laboratory training activities. These laboratory-seminars start at the top and gradually move down through the whole organization.

Phase 2. The behavior dynamics of existing organizational groups are studied. This is the team-development phase.

Phase 3. The experience of the preceding phase is extended to include the interworkings of organizational units which must cooperate and achieve coordination of effort. Intergroup confrontation meetings are used at the major group/group interfaces.

Phase 4. An *ideal strategic corporate model* is developed by the top-level team with the assistance of other groups. This model deals with the processes, structure, and culture of the organization.

Phase 5. Implementation tactics are developed to move the company toward the ideal strategic corporate model. Temporary task forces are used as the medium for this purpose.

Phase 6. Changes are measured from before Phase 1 to after Phase 5 in order to stabilize at a more effective level of functioning.

In the Blake and Mouton approach the initial phases utilize the techniques of T-grouping, laboratory training, or sensitivity training. Recently this list of techniques has been extended to include more drastic encounter and gestalt therapy procedures. The objective is to condition motives, attitudes, and values to produce a receptivity to the ideal corporate model of later phases. This corporate model invariably involves some degree of commitment to participative management. It may involve a highly participative version of management by objectives. Thus, Professor Thomas Patten, of Michigan State University, writes, "An MBO-OD installation and implementation moves an organization from one in which authoritarian styles prevail to one which is more open, trusting, human, and rewarding . . . . Theory Y managerial styles and assumptions and employee participation in decision-making . . . ."

Other features which may well characterize the *ideal strategic corporate model* are large spans of control, so that a manager cannot supervise all his subordinates closely and make decisions himself; decentralization of decisionmaking to the lowest possible point in the organization; flat managerial hierarchies, with very few levels; linking-pin, or overlapping, group structure, which views the organization as a series of teams with interlocking representatives; integration of planning with performance, so that an individual plans his own work; extensive use of project teams, committees, and similar temporary groups; job enrichment, whereby an individual takes over many of the duties and much of the discretionary power of his superior; abolition of formal job analysis; reduced downward communication and increased horizontal and two-way vertical communication; merging of line and staff; substitution of informal organization for much of the formal; and ultimately the elimination of hierarchic control procedures, with group sources of control being substituted.

The key assumption of the Blake and Mouton approach is, as Michael Beer, of Corning Glass Works, points out, ". . . that organization change must start with individual change as the unfreezing mechanism, and that process problems at the interpersonal, group and intergroup levels must be dealt with before changes in strategy and the organization's internal environment can take place." Dr. Beer himself feels that his sequencing is not essential, and that a move to the new structures can be taken first, with the reeducation process following. In any event, it is clear that a comprehensive organization development effort includes some combination of laboratory training, to change attitudes and values, and extensive reorganizing (renewal), in order to consolidate the shift from hierarchic to group bases of control.

The New Values

The values of organization development are democratic rather than authoritarian, humanistic rather than highly rational and pragmatic, egalitarian rather than hierarchic. Key terms and concepts are authenticity, trust, confrontation, collaboration, growth, team building, human development, intervention, openness, family group, attitude feedback, individual worth, action research, organizational renewal, organic systems, understanding, interpersonal competence, cooperation, human process consultation, transactional, third-party peacemaking, expressing feelings, free communication, socioemotional process, and sensitivity to needs. Again and again in these words there is an expression of concern for the individual, of the desirability of harmonious group relationships and the free expression of feelings, and of a perceived need for change in existing organizations.

Professors Wendell French and Cecil Bell, of the University of Washington, in one of the most recent books on the topic, differentiate organization development in terms of its emphasis on:

- *group* and organizational processes
- the work *team* as the key unit for learning
- *collaborative* management of work-team culture
- management of the *culture* of the total system
- *action* research
- behavioral science *change* agents
- a view of the *change* effort as an ongoing process
- primary emphasis on *human* and social relationships

The key words appear to be *group, team, collaborative* (read participative), *culture* (and cultural values), *action, change,* and *human* relations.

Professor Robert Golembiewski, of the University of Georgia, extends this view with regard to existing organizational forms. "OD programs will at least increasingly challenge these centers of power to become more open to a wide variety of influence attempts. Indeed, an OD program may fundamentally alter the distribution of power." At another point he says, "It is not overly dramatic to describe the common goals of OD efforts as moving toward the nonbureaucratic organization, or perhaps even toward antibureaucracy." He subscribes to the following values as consistent with organization development:

- full and free communication
- greater reliance on open confrontation in managing conflict . . . as contrasted with a reliance on coercion or compromise
- influence based on competence rather than personal whim or formal power
- expression of emotional as well as task-oriented behavior
- acceptance of conflict between the individual and his organization

What emerges from these various writers as the thrust of OD is the following:

- a more democratic or participative set of values which is antihierarchy, antibureaucracy, antiauthoritarian, and antiauthority.
- a greater orientation to and consciousness of the immediate peer and work groups and a commitment to group sources of control.
- less individual competitiveness and less use of power by established authority; this has been called power equalization and is reflected in the emphasis on collaboration.
- more stress on openness and free expression of feelings
- an emphasis on individual goals at the expense of organizational goals; humanism in the extreme.

Given these values, it is not surprising that organization development is out to *change* existing business organizations and to engage in an *ongoing* change process. This is nothing less than an all-out onslaught on the existing business system. The questions which remain are: Is this onslaught justified? Is there any likelihood that this approach will work? How will such an approach relate to the managerial talent shortage problem?

OD Values and the New Generation

Professors Friedlander and Brown state, "OD as a field is faced with decisions about the balance it can and will strike between changing institutions to increase human development and changing people to promote institutional development. The two goals are rarely consistent with each other." There is a realism in this statement that is all too rare in the field. Furthermore, Friedlander and Brown clearly remain uncertain on what that balance should be. Yet many other writers are not; a sizable number favor changing institutions to accommodate their version of human development. This appears to be in part an outgrowth of America's "affluent society," which at least for the moment can afford such experimentation. However, strong supportive pressures of a very similar kind come from the values and attitudes of the new generation and the youth culture.

My point is this: Somehow the values of organization development and the values increasingly prevalent on campuses and among the upcoming generation of managers have coalesced around the same themes. These two threads inevitably are destined to meet in the halls of corporate headquarters and the offices of plant managers. Both sets of values are concerned with group control, free emotional expression, anti-authority behavior, and the like. Put more bluntly, organization development appears to have the potential for accelerating the attitudinal, value, and motivational changes that have contributed to the current threat of managerial talent shortages. Rather than solving the problem, organization development gives every promise of making it worse.

This assumes, of course, that organization development does work to achieve its goals and inculcate its values and that the organizational form finally achieved is one which still requires motivation to manage. On the first point there is now little question. To the extent that an organization development program includes some version of laboratory training, and most programs do, there is a good chance that humanistic values will take hold and have an effect on a sizable number of participants. There has been a good deal of research in this area which has been reviewed by Professor Golembiewski and others. All conclude that laboratory training, T-groups, and the like do have the potential for changing people. This does not mean that all organization development programs achieve such changes. But when change does occur it can be expected to take the form of reduced authoritarianism, increased independence, greater moral relativism, stronger group identifications, more opposition to authority, less controlling of emotional expression, and the more pronounced social concern that humanism implies. Most of these are characteristics which have also been identified as typifying the younger generation, although there are some additional aspects of the change on campus that do not also appear to be consequences of laboratory training.

Organization Development and the Organization

The two major components of organization development are (1) some type of laboratory training, and (2) the creation and implementation of what Blake and Mouton call the *ideal strategic corporate model,* i.e., organization renewal. We know that the first component may result in changed motives, attitudes, and values. In the absence of the second component these changes can mean serious trouble for the kind of organization that needs motivation to manage. Such trouble has become a reality for a number of firms already, because in a number of instances organization development efforts have progressed only as far as Phase 3 in the Blake and Mouton sequence. What happens is that the new OD-based value system comes in conflict with the existing value structure. Since the existing value structure is supported by long-standing policies, procedures, organizational forms, and authority relationships, it tends to hold fast, but there is also a decreased motivation to manage, increased internal dissension, and often, in the long run, a massive managerial exodus. In a period of preoccupation with such value conflicts, most companies are not likely to operate very effectively.

This means that a company that undertakes organization development should be prepared to go all the way, and adopt an *ideal strategic corporate model* with all that is implied in terms of changes in the locus of control, and thus bring itself into alignment with the OD-based values. To do otherwise verges on organizational suicide. The trouble is that going all the way with organization development may have much the same result. The cause of the demise is different, but the result may well be the same.

One problem is that although there is an abundance of research dealing with laboratory training, there is practically none dealing with a comprehensive, full-scale organization development effort. Professors Friedlander and Brown comment, "We simply do not know much about whether OD interventions lead to better management of intergroup relations or not . . . There is very little systematic research . . . ." Dr. Beer notes, "Organization development is still in its infancy and to date little research on its effectiveness exists." These statements derive from two very recent and highly competent attempts to review and evaluate the literature and current practice in the organization development field.

Although there have been some case reports of highly successful organization development efforts, these studies suffer from the same deficiencies that characterized the early research on participative management. It is not possible to tell, given the way the research was conducted, what caused the changes. Having been burned once as a result of premature optimism, even many who are highly committed to organization development and to humanist values are not yet willing to say their approach has proven itself at the bar of scientific research. This means that those who do undertake an organization development effort are assuming some risk. It is important, accordingly, to look into the data that do exist for the purpose of identifying these risks and determining what negative consequences, if any, might be anticipated.

Contraindications to OD

All that was said regarding participative management in Chapter 11 applies to organization development with equal force. In fact, organization development may be viewed as one type of strategy for actually moving an organization from a hierarchic to a group control system. The utilization of some kind of laboratory training as an essential aspect of the change process distinguishes organization development from participative management per se, however, and certain additional risks inhere in the use of this particular approach.

Research conducted by Professors Samuel Deep, Bernard Bass, and James Vaughn, at the University of Pittsburgh, leads to the conclusion that organization development can produce an excess of confidence in each other's dependability among group members. Everyone is confident that each person will do his share on his own, controls are relaxed, and in the end the group does not organize to do its work, with the result that performance falters. Such failure of group control may not be an inevitable consequence, but it does represent a risk.

The importance of the effects of organization development on output factors such as productivity and profit is emphasized by another study conducted by Professors Reed Powell and John Stinson, of Ohio State University. They, too, found that the consequence of a program of the organization development type was a decrease in effectiveness and profit performance. Here, the failure was attributed to an abdication of leadership occasioned by the laboratory training, coupled with insufficient development of group control, at least insofar as getting the work out is concerned. There appears to have been a move to *laissez-faire* rather than effective group control with the elimination of hierarchic authority. In view of the serious questions raised regarding productivity under participative management generally, this research related more directly to organization development takes on added significance.

Other questions have to do with the effects of laboratory and encounter procedures on group members. In a recent book entitled *The Encounter Game*, Dr. Bruce Maliver documents in considerable detail the adverse effects of the encounter experience on individual participants. His descriptions of cases where emotional problems have resulted are often chillingly explicit. In his view the encounter movement represents a bastardization of humanistic principles which has hedonism as its implicit ethic. He sees no relation between the encounter approach and the achievement of corporate goals.

Although the applications of encounter techniques described by Dr. Maliver tend to be extreme, relative to what is usually included in an organization development program, such applications are not unheard of on the corporate scene. A recent article by Louis Allen, a management consultant with long experience in this area, emphasizes the fact that laboratory training in any form can well be detrimental to productivity and act in opposition to the goals of profitmaking organizations. This article, as well as Dr. Maliver's book, should be required reading for anyone considering undertaking the risks of a long-range organization development program. It is well to be informed, even if one ultimately decides in favor of organization development.

The OD Strategy

My own conclusion, based on the evidence, remains rather simple. I do believe that there are circumstances under which some move toward particpative management is justified, both to handle internal sources of dissatisfaction and to reduce the need for motivation to manage when it is in short supply. However, at this time it seems to me that the risks involved in adopting organization development as a means of implementing such a participative approach are too great. This assumes of course that organization development would involve what has been described as one of its major components — a technique known as, or akin to, sensitivity training, T-grouping, growth laboratory, communications laboratory, encounter sessions, gestalt therapy, and so on. The very number of aliases raises doubts. There is no "one best way" to manage and humanism is clearly not such a best way in any event. To the extent that organization development advocates the humanistic view it must remain suspect in the corporate setting.

The current situation with respect to OD is reminiscent of the findings in an earlier period with another approach. A number of years ago the Bell System instituted an extensive program of education in the humanities at the University of Pennsylvania and elsewhere, with a view to the broadening and intellectual enrichment of its executives. A careful evaluation study conducted by Professor Morris Viteles, of the same school, indicated that those exposed to the program experienced a ripening of artistic values and a greater acceptance of aesthetic values, while at the same time coming to value practical economic activities less. Furthermore, their attitudes shifted from the more conservative pole to a greater radicalism. There is every reason to believe that these unanticipated consequences produced executives who were less involved in their work and less involved in the economic goals of their company.

The problem is that approaches such as these are sold to management by individuals who have as their personal goals something quite different from company profit performance. They want to change the world in some other image, and they have techniques designed to accomplish this. This does not mean that participative management and even organization development should be rejected entirely, but it does mean that they should be evaluated objectively and never given free reign entirely independent of hierarchic control.

13

Variable Structuring

As I have indicated, a structural approach to solving human-resource problems, in contrast to a more technological approach, does offer some promise. A company faced with the prospect of dwindling supplies of managerial talent occasioned by reduced levels of motivation to manage can use certain structural changes to reduce its need for such talent. Basically this approach involves substituting other bases of control for the hierarchic in those parts of the firm and in those decision areas where this appears feasible.

What I am recommending should not be construed as involving an overall reduction in control within the company. Instead it is a strategy of carefully considered, differential substitution of types of control which do not require motivation to manage for hierarchic control, which does require motivation to manage. The limits to this approach are clearly established by the nature of the company workforce and the requirements of the particular business. Some firms may not be able to go very far with it; no company should consider anything approaching a total elimination of hierarchy. But there is the possibility of reducing the need for motivation to manage here, and of at least partially neutralizing the conflict potential inherent in pressures for participatory democracy from younger managers and workers as well.

The Specifics of Variable Structuring

Effective utilization of the variable-structuring strategy as a means of dealing with managerial talent shortages requires a clear perception of when various types of control are feasible. Although current knowledge in this area is far from being all that could be desired, some guidelines are available.

Professional control assumes the existence of a sizable professional component within the company. Examples would be a corporate legal department or a scientific research unit. However, many other groups might qualify for the professional designation, depending on the particular company involved. There is considerable disagreement regarding the defining characteristics of a profession, and it is compounded by the fact that a numer of occupations are currently aspiring to professional status. Accordingly, it is important to be clear on when professional control can be relied upon to operate effectively.

One condition is that there be a set of specialized techniques and a body of relevant knowledge learned through some relatively standardized educational process. As part of this educational process the professional-to-be also learns certain norms and adopts as his own certain expected behaviors. In addition, there must be an association of colleagues (the professional association or society) which supports and influences the careers of members. Among other things this association typically sets forth certain ethical requirements and standards of practice. Finally, society at large must recognize the professional's status and define certain people as being members of the profession. A person must not be able to escape the pressures of professional control by contending he is not really a member of the profession.

In the professional context, pressures from the training experience, from the professional association, and from colleagues do control behavior. Furthermore, authority automatically accrues to the more experienced, more expert members of the profession, so that they are likely to assume a leadership role even without formal designation. In such a situation, hierarchic control is not needed and motivation to manage does not appear to be an essential ingredient of success. Support personnel, such as technicians, clerical workers, those concerned with financial matters, and the like are automatically subordinated to the dominant professional group because they are less expert in the particular field. Decisions arise out of consensus among the professionals, but are strongly influenced by the senior, more respected, and more expert members.

In this situation, the duties normally handled at the lower levels of a managerial hierarchy can be assumed by the professional control process, and managers with a strong will to manage are not needed. They may even present a problem, because superimposing hierarchic on professional control produces an excessive amount of restriction. On the other hand, it is not possible to assume that what is good for the profession is always good for the company. In certain areas such congruence may exist, but rarely in all. Thus, I believe an overarching hierarchic control and motivation to manage must be retained in order to establish limits on the various professional components. But within the professional group itself the appointment of individuals to positions at various levels of management might well be dispensed with. Awards of professional status, along the lines of the academic ladder of professorial ranks in a university, can be made by the group itself.

Group control differs from professional control in a number of respects, with one of the most important being the lack of an outside referent. It seems to me that the group approach can operate effectively only within relatively small, homogeneous units which are not required to coordinate their activities and decisions with other parts of the organization on a continuous basis. Examples of what I have in mind are sales districts or regions, branch banks, small highly automated manufacturing facilities, and the like. Either the group members must have roughly equal amounts of expertise in the area of operation, or different members should be expert in different aspects. In any event, one individual's expertise should not so dominate the group that group control is effectively lost.

It is important that face-to-face meetings and decision making by consensus or by the majority operate to produce a highly cohesive and unified group. Leadership should be "emergent" in the sense that the group structures itself to perform its duties. Thus, instead of a particular person being put in charge by higher authority, the group itself should either formally designate such a person or informally act toward a given individual as if he were in charge. Often under these circumstances different leaders emerge for different purposes.

In such situations there is always the threat of *laissez-faire* occurring, with each individual going off in his own direction, and group control failing to develop. This is less likely to happen to the extent that all members spend time talking to each other about the work to be done. For this reason large units cannot exercise effective group control; people keep getting lost to the group or so much time is devoted to groupwork and maintenance of group membership that the job to be done gets only secondary attention.

Furthermore, group control operates at its best in situations where membership is stable — where the group can get itself organized, establish methods of control, and then go about its work knowing that its control system has widespread acceptance in the group because all have participated in developing it. This approach is not appropriate where turnover is high or where there are large numbers of temporary workers. I do not believe it is feasible to use it with temporary project teams either, unless the project has an expected duration of several years. Group control can be just as unpleasant to members as hierarchic control. If people know that they will escape this control shortly when the group disbands, they may well refuse to accept its dictates in the here and now. Thus, a short-term project team is very likely to degenerate into *laissez-faire.*

As with professional units, those operating under group control do have to be tied into the larger organization in some manner. There has to be some method of protecting against *laissez-faire* and some method of keeping group efforts in tune with the goals of the company as a whole. This means that once again some kind of overarching umbrella of hierarchic control must be retained. At this point top-level motivation to manage comes back in the picture; in fact, it becomes even more important than it was before group control was initiated. However, within the unit involved, motivation to manage is replaced to a large extent by group decision making and group pressures for compliance.

Task control is much more of an unknown quantity, largely because it has been studied relatively little, and it is this very fact that leads me to question its use on anything but a limited basis at present. There simply is not enough information available on the effectiveness of task control to warrant instituting it as a replacement for hierarchic control in any sizable segment of a company. Yet it is important to be aware of this alternative because research may ultimately provide the needed information about it.

It appears that task control can operate in two ways. One is by "push," as when customers crowd around a sales clerk to be waited on. The clerk may well work very hard under such circumstances merely to meet the demand. There is no need for hierarchic control by a supervisor because the customers provide a control which is inherent in the task. In another context, the operation of machinery may accomplish the same thing. The problem with this "push" control is that, although it tends to keep people working at appropriate tasks when they are on the job, it does not keep them on the job. In fact it may drive them away from the job situation to avoid the pressure.

This suggests that effective task control should include a "pull" element which attracts people to the job and makes them want to perform in it. The vertical job-enlargement or job-enrichment procedures and research reported by Robert Ford, of AT&T, come to mind. Under this approach, the work itself is made more satisfying by including in each job more of what would otherwise be done by a supervisor — planning, quality control, and the like.

Yet it is now apparent that job enrichment is much more effective in motivating some people than others. Utilizing task control may thus require not only the achievement of a delicate balance between "push" and "pull" factors in the work, but the selection of people who can in fact perform well with relatively little control other than that inherent in the job itself. Based on current evidence it would be foolhardy to conclude that all people can do this.

Ultimately I believe it will be possible to establish certain work units where neither hierarchic nor group nor professional control is needed and where the individual works in response to the push and pull of the work itself, much as the traditional entrepreneur is said to do. However, it seems unlikely that the majority of jobs can be designed this way, and even less likely that the majority of people will respond well to this type of control. Furthermore, far too little is known in this area as yet, in spite of some rather grandiose claims for the job-enrichment approach. Consequently, the extent to which the demand for motivation to manage can be alleviated by substituting task for herierarchic control appears at present to be less than for either professional or group control.

Retention of Hierarchic Control

Based on the evidence now available, it seems to me that a resort to variable structuring still requires the retention of hierarchic control and the will to manage in many sectors of a company of any size. This would be true in any component where large groups of people must work together at relatively routine tasks, as in the core manufacturing operations of a consumer-goods producer or the core clerical activities of a large bank or insurance company.

I also believe that some degree of hierarchic control must be retained in the relationship between top management and the rest of the company in order to keep all segments of the company oriented toward performance and profit goals. Yet the way in which this control is exercised will have to differ considerably depending on the type of control operating at lower levels. The light but firm rein required in those areas where professional, group, or even task control has been instituted differs considerably from the more heavy-handed approach required where hierarchic control remains supreme. Variable structuring requires highly differentiated treatment of various organizational units by top management, but it continues to call for high levels of the will to manage at the top — if only because hierarchic control is also retained there.

Furthermore, there is reason to believe that computerized information systems may help to solve one of the most persistent problems of hierarchic control — the tendency for upward communication to become distorted. A pioneering study by Professor John Athanassiades, of Georgia State University, demonstrates clearly that such distortion is greater under hierarchic control than under professional control, and that it is greater when members at lower levels are threatened and insecure. The distortion appears to represent an attempt on the part of those who are subject to hierarchic control to present themselves in the most favorable light.

It would seem possible now, or in the near future, to design computer systems which would severely limit the possibilities for distortion in upward communication, merely because information can be moved from its point of origin up to the place where it is needed without passing through a human chain, each link of which represents a potential distortion point. Such computer systems may be well serve to increase threat and insecurity, because of the difficulty of influencing them, but they should yield more valid information to top management.

Project and Matrix Structures

The relationship between project management, whether utilized as the primary basis of organization or as an overlay on existing structures, and the need for motivation to manage is a complex one. Under certain circumstances a project-management approach may serve to increase the need for managerial motivation, thus intensifying the talent crunch; under other circumstances it may be a useful aspect of the variable structuring strategy.

Under project management the organizational units are formed on an ad hoc, temporary basis — to produce a weapons system, build a bridge, or develop a new product. There is a definite objective, and when this is accomplished the particular unit disbands. The size of the project unit varies. In aerospace and construction all individuals needed to complete the project typically are assigned directly to it, being phased in and out as their skills are needed. They may or may not have membership in another unit while working on the project. In other industries the actual project unit tends to be small; additional resources are drawn from the outside as needed.

There is a strong emphasis on direct horizontal communications between specialists rather than on vertical communications through the hierarchy. In industries such as aerospace and construction, and in management consulting, the project unit operates largely as a team. These teams may well contain members from more than one organization; consulting engagement teams often include representatives from the client company as well as from the consulting firm.

The actual authority of project managers over decisions varies from almost complete control of matters relevant to the project to mere persuasion. In the matrix structure primary control may be retained in the base department rather than in the project, or it may be split between the two. (These varied relationships are elaborated in considerable detail in the book *Industrial Project Management* by Professors George Steiner, of the University of California, Los Angeles, and William Ryan, of Indiana University.) Under certain circumstances group or professional control may be utilized.

One of the major difficulties with project management is that sources of control may become so splintered and ambiguous that the situation disintegrates toward *laissez-faire*, with individual members going their own ways quite independent of organizational requirements. Because of this tendency inherent in the project form, it becomes very important to establish sources of control clearly.

Yet research conducted by Professor Clayton Reeser, of the University of Hawaii, indicates that here control also can become excessive. When hierarchic control resides both in the project manager and in the line relationship, as in certain matrix structures, a project member can be overcontrolled. Furthermore, this approach involves two managers instead of one, thus increasing the demand for motivation to manage. On a number of counts, then, the use of split hierarchic control in a matrix structure does not appear to recommend itself.

On the other hand, where the project manager operates as a persuader, integrator, and facilitator he can be extremely effective without being a source of control. His skills are interpersonal and his major function is to foster horizontal communication where it is needed. Motivation to manage is irrelevant. Hierarchic control is exercised through the regular organization structure.

Alternatively, hierarchic control may be shifted almost entirely to the project manager, as Professor Jay Galbraith has advocated. Under this approach, personnel assignments are made almost entirely to the project, and authority over decisions and budgets resides there as well. Here managerial motivation is important in the project manager, but the need for other types of managers outside the project is drastically reduced.

The problem with strategies either minimizing or maximizing hierarchic control through the project manager is that although they do not increase the need for motivation to manage they do not reduce it either. Thus, they have little value as solutions for the managerial talent shortage, whatever their value on other grounds.

However, the project form does appear to be particularly suited to both professional and group sources of control. Where the project utilizes large numbers of professionals, as with a scientific research program or a legal task force, professional control can easily be utilized, with the project manager operating entirely on the basis of expert power. Such a manager serves at the pleasure of the dominant professional group, and nonprofessional tasks are handled by individuals who must respond to the professional consensus. As long as the project team does not become so large that it must contain a disproportionate number of individuals who are not members of the dominant profession, this type of project effort can contribute to solving the problem created by declining supplies of managerial motivation. It is a form of variable structuring.

The use of group project control also seems feasible where a dominant professional group does not exist. As previously indicated, the project must be of considerable duration, the project team not very large in numbers, and stability of membership a characteristic. Such project units require loose-rein hierarchic control from upper levels of management to keep them on course, as do professionally controlled project units.

Whether or not a given company can utilize the variable-structuring strategy, with project units controlled by professional and group pressures, depends largely on the nature of the business. The project approach is generally considered most appropriate to high-technology, research-oriented contexts where flexibility and problem-solving are essential. Such contexts should also be most amenable to professional and group control. In other situations hierarchic control may remain essential, whether the project form is used or not.

Entrepreneurship Through Venture Teams

Although the feasibility of using task control in the project context generally remains just as uncertain as in other contexts, there is one area where such an approach appears promising. This is the area of corporate entrepreneurship or venture management. In activities of this kind, there appears to be a good possibility that task control can be substituted for hierarchic control, and other motives for the will to manage.

To understand what is involved here it is important to know something about what makes for successful entrepreneurship generally. A very respectable body of research now indicates that achievement motivation is a major factor in effective entrepreneurship, much more so than in corporate managerial success. Small firms founded by individuals with strong achievement drives are more likely to prosper than those founded by less achievement-oriented people.

Second, an extensive study of successful entrepreneurs in Michigan, conducted by Professors Orvis Collins and David Moore, indicates that these are people who are very unresponsive to hierarchic types of control. They do not gravitate to hierarchically controlled organizations very often, and they tend to do poorly there when they do; yet they usually do well on their own with their own companies. The control here derives from the task. They have to work hard and effectively because the company will fail if they do not, and they are "pulled" onward to greater effort by the anticipation of making it on their own and of sizable rewards. This is an ideal "push and pull" context of the kind that makes task control work best.

These research findings suggest that if companies want to develop new ventures along entrepreneurial lines they can use task control. Furthermore, they can and should then staff these venture teams with people of a kind that do not usually exist in the parent company, and who if they do are likely to be having problems as managers, probably being viewed as too uncooperative and independent, perhaps even as selfish and untrustworthy.

Such pro-achievement, antihierarchy individuals may well also be in declining supply at present, just as those with high managerial motivation are. At least that is the conclusion of Professor David McClelland. Furthermore, there probably is an overlap between achievement motivation and managerial motivation, with the two having some tendency to be found together in the same person. However, there clearly is a pool of entrepreneurial talent that is typically not available to large companies, and which might be used to substitute for motivation to manage under conditions of task rather than hierarchic control.

In order to make this approach work, companies will have to locate the right kinds of people and set them up in business by providing the capital, but very little else. The control of the marketplace, rather than the control of the boardroom, must be permitted to operate. The new venture must be allowed to fail if necessary, as well as to succeed handsomely. If a decision is made to shift to corporate hierarchic control, the original entrepreneur or entrepreneurs will probably have to be removed, perhaps to start another venture. Ultimately, should the new venture be highly successful and grow to considerable size, this kind of shift will have to be made if the new organization is to be managed effectively and integrated into the parent structure. But in the period of early growth, task control in a project-type context can be used to reduce the need for motivation to manage.

The major problems with this strategy appear to be in the area of staffing and in relinquishing control to the entrepreneurial task. A recent study by Professors James Hlavacek, of the State University of New York at Albany, and Victor Thompson, of the University of Florida, indicates that venture-team managers do tend to be less subject to the typical corporate hierarchic controls than project managers. However, a parallel study by Professors David Wilemon and Gary Gemmill, of Syracuse University, makes it clear that a sizable amount of hierarchic control often remains, with venture managers being forced to utilize corporate resources and deal with other corporate managers as "insiders with little power" rather than as outsiders buying products and services. Often, even if the right kind of venture manager is selected, continued hierarchic control spells continued conflict and misdirected effort. Yet selection in favor of a better corporate fit spells failure for the new venture. One does best to go all the way with the task-oriented achievement-motivation formula, or else to stick entirely with the hierarchically controlled managerial-motivation approach. The latter, however, does nothing to alleviate managerial talent shortages, while the former does have this potential.

Basically what emerges is that a carefully thought-out movement to variable structuring, whether in the project form or not, can yield a reduced demand for managerial motivation, which may or may not match the reduction in supply of managerial talent, depending on the particular business involved. On the other hand, I personally remain very uncertain about the value of using group and task-control procedures in the absence of the justifying impact of shortages in managerial motivation. The use of professional control and expert power in the hands of senior professionals has in a sense been validated. We know it can work. Group and task control have many pluses and minuses, and in the latter case a number of uncertainties as well. Given a shortage of the motivation to manage required by hierarchic control, group and task control may well work to solve that problem under certain circumstances. Group control in small, isolated units, and task control in the entrepreneurial context — these do seem feasible. But overardent devotees should be treated with considerable skepticism. Hierarchy has proved itself in many situations. We should not throw it away without knowing for sure that we have something better.

14

Managerial Role-Motivation Training

Professor Leavitt describes three types of mediator process which may serve to bring about change in organizations. In preceding chapters we have considered strategies for solving problems of managerial talent shortage based on two of these approaches — the technological and the structural. The people approach remains to be considered. This approach emphasizes changing people while leaving the technology and structure of the organization unaltered.

Actually, organization development is a compound procedure with elements of both the structural and people approaches, although the ultimate result is a major structural reorganization. However, organization development does not appear to offer a meaningful solution to managerial manpower problems, and it clearly is not a people approach which accepts existing hierarchic control structures as given. A more direct people approach, which focuses specifically on changing individuals to make them function more effectively as managers within existing hierarchic control systems, is managerial role-motivation training.

Training Procedures and Content

Managerial role-motivation training utilizes conventional lecture and lecture-discussion teaching techniques; thus its procedures are largely the antithesis of those employed in T-groups and laboratory training. Typically, training sessions are held once a week, although they may be more frequent. Each session lasts an hour or longer, and the training extends over a period of several months. The total teaching time usually is between twenty and thirty hours. The size of the groups undergoing training has varied from about ten to as many as one hundred.

The content of training is such that the instructor must be knowledgeable in the social sciences and, in particular, in the field of psychology. The lecture material concentrates on the various reasons why a subordinate might fail to perform effectively in the work situation. The material is presented in such a way as to give the participants a feeling of being in a position of responsibility, faced with the necessity of having to diagnose the reasons behind the performance failure of a subordinate in order to take appropriate remedial action. Thus the demands, challenges, and satisfactions of the managerial role are constantly reiterated. The following brief topical outline for a ten-session program provides an overview of the subjects covered:

Lecture 1: Ineffective management; a definition of ineffective performance.

Lecture 2: Physical illness and job performance; physical disorders of emotional origin; physical characteristics and job performance; theory of intelligence; the relationship between intelligence and performance; procedures for improving performance where intelligence is a factor in failure.

Lecture 3: The nature of emotional disorder; emotions and performance; correction and treatment where emotions are strategic for ineffective performance; alcoholism.

Lecture 4: Aspects of human motivation; fear of failure and pleasure in success; other motives affecting performance; general and specific work motivation; dealing with motivational problems.

Lecture 5: Family crises; separation from the family; the predominance of family considerations over work demands; the possibilities for managerial action where family factors have contributed to job failure.

Lecture 6: The cohesion of the work group; inducing a positive group impact on performance.

Lecture 7: Insufficient organizational action as a cause of failure; personnel placement policies; organizational overpermissiveness; intracompany conflict and organizational failure.

Lecture 8: The nature of cultural values; the relationship between values and job performance; specific values influencing those who fail; possible types of managerial action where cultural values are strategic.

Lecture 9: Economic forces and job failure; geographic location of work and failure; the physical working environment; danger and the accident prone; subjective danger situations.

Lecture 10: The managerial job as a subjective danger situation; subjective danger and managerial performance.

The objectives of this training are twofold:

1. The quite obvious goal of helping managers to deal more effectively with deficiencies in the work performance of their subordinates, however caused, and

2. the less apparent goal of developing motivation to manage in all of its aspects.

It is the latter objective that makes managerial role-motivation training a topic for consideration here. If the training does achieve what is intended, then it can contribute to resolving the managerial talent shortage by increasing the amount of motivation to manage. Such a strategy has considerable appeal either as a supplement to approaches aimed at reducing the demand for managerial talent, like variable structuring, or as an alternative to them. The crucial question then is: Does it work?

Does managerial role-motivation training actually increase motivation to manage and produce more effective managerial performance?

Change in an R & D Department

Over the last fifteen years, several of my former students and I have done a considerable amount of research with the objective of finding out about the change-producing capabilities of the role-motivation approach. Although there are still many things that we do not know about it, one thing can be said with certainty: Like laboratory or sensitivity training, managerial role-motivation training *can* change people.

The original study contributing to this conclusion was done in the R&D department of a major oil company. I taught the course and seventy-two managers completed it. There were four groups of approximately equal size, so that if a manager was unable to attend with his regular group he could still come to another session at another time during the week. Thus, attendance was good.

Of the seventy-two managers involved, fifty-six were induced to complete a questionnaire measuring motivation to manage both as the training was beginning and again shortly after it was completed. We hoped that on the average the level of their motivation would increase, and in fact it did; 59 percent had higher scores the second time. The major changes, insofar as aspects of motivation to manage are concerned, were in the development of more favorable attitudes toward authority, a greater desire to compete, a more pronounced desire to exercise power, and a greater sense of responsibility.

The research design called for a second group of managers who did not take the course to complete the same questionnaire at the same time as the trained managers did. The idea was to determine if changes might be caused by factors quite independent of the training — merely completing the questionnaire twice, for instance, or experiencing an event that influenced everybody in the R&D department. The results obtained with this group of thirty untrained managers served to reinforce the conclusion that managerial role-motivation training works. Without training there was no indication of any meaningful increase in motivation to manage; in fact on some of the specific aspects there appeared to be an overall decrease. In contrast to the 59 percent with higher motivation scores in the trained group, only 17 percent without training showed any increase.

This kind of study is fine as far as it goes; it does give evidence that a sizable number of managers were stimulated to increased managerial motivation. But the really important question has to do with whether such changes are retained over the years and result in real behavior change, so that the person actually does become a better manager. This point has been made most effectively by Wallace Wohlking, of the New York State School of Industrial and Labor Relations at Cornell University, whose practical experience as a training consultant leads him to question the efficiency of many management development programs.

To look into this matter two groups of managers in the R&D department were compared. The first group was drawn from the seventy-two managers who had been given the role-motivation training. Since the concern was to identify improved *managers*, this group was reduced to fifty-two by eliminating all those who subsequently went on to careers primarily in scientific research, as senior scientists and the like. The second comparison group similarly was selected from those managers who were in the department at the time the training was conducted but who did not participate in the training. This group numbered forty-nine.

The two groups were made up of managers at almost identical average levels in the company hierarchy at the time of the training. On a scale where the lowest managerial grade was 7 and the highest 18, both groups averaged between 11.5 and 12.0. Furthermore, management appraisal ratings of advancement potential at that time also indicated that the groups were equal. On the 4-point rating scale used, both groups had an average of 2.9; 1.0 was the highest possible rating. All other things being equal, the two groups should have produced approximately equal numbers of good managers over the years ensuing after training. Of course, the crucial question is whether all things were equal or whether the training made a difference.

EXHIBIT 34
Effects of Managerial Role-Motivation Training on
Motivation to Manage in an R & D Department

	Managers Who Underwent Training		Untrained Managers	
Motivation to Manage	Before	After	Before	After
High Motivation	23 (41%)	34 (61%)	15 (50%)	15 (50%)
Low Motivation	33 (59%)	22 (39%)	15 (50%)	15 (50%)
Favorable Attitude Toward Authority				
High Motivation	19 (34%)	26 (46%)	16 (53%)	17 (57%)
Low Motivation	37 (66%)	30 (54%)	14 (47%)	13 (43%)
Desire to Compete				
High Motivation	29 (52%)	34 (61%)	21 (70%)	15 (50%)
Low Motivation	27 (48%)	22 (39%)	9 (30%)	15 (50%)
Desire to Exercise Power				
High Motivation	29 (52%)	36 (64%)	15 (50%)	15 (50%)
Low Motivation	27 (48%)	20 (36%)	15 (50%)	15 (50%)
Sense of Responsibility				
High Motivation	21 (37%)	28 (50%)	13 (43%)	9 (30%)
Low Motivation	35 (63%)	28 (50%)	17 (57%)	21 (70%)

Five years after the training program I went back and looked up the records of these 101 managers. Among the 75 still employed by the company, promotions were much more frequent in the trained group. All the demotions and the great majority of the cases where no grade change had occurred were in the untrained group. Assuming that people are promoted in this kind of situation because they are behaving and performing more effectively as managers, there is no question that the training did make a difference.

EXHIBIT 35
Effects of Managerial Role-Motivation Training on
Later Success in an R & D Department

Promotions over next five years for those who stayed that long	Managers Who Underwent Training	Untrained Managers
Promoted 3 or more grade levels	10 (28%)	8 (21%)
Promoted 1 or 2 grade levels	21 (58%)	14 (36%)
No grade level change	5 (14%)	13 (33%)
Demoted	0 (0%)	4 (10%)
Performance appraisals at the time of separation for those who left during next five years		
Recommended for rehiring	11 (69%)	3 (30%)
Recommendation against rehiring	5 (31%)	7 (70%)
Promoted or recommended for rehiring	42 (81%)	25 (51%)
Not promoted or recommendation against rehiring	10 (19%)	24 (49%)
Average grade level before training	11.6	11.8
Average appraised potential before training	2.9	2.9

Among the twenty-six managers who left the company within the five-year period, the evidence of better performance in the trained group is equally strong. Because a rather large number left in a short time period, promotion rates could not be used to demonstrate managerial success. However, in all twenty-six cases the immediate superiors had provided a notation in the personnel records as to whether they would rehire the particular manager if he wanted to come back. A vote against rehiring strongly suggests that the man was fired. In this context, also, the trained managers emerged as far superior to the untrained. Taking the followup group as a whole, there is no question that those who experienced managerial role-motivation training were more likely to have experienced success subsequently as managers. In short, all the data available on this group of managers seems to indicate the positive impact of the training. I say this with full realization that it is possible that other, unknown factors may account for the results. In my own mind, however, I feel this is very unlikely.

Change Among Business Administration Students

More recent studies of the effects of managerial role-motivation training have been carried out with business administration students. The most comprehensive of these were conducted at the University of Oregon. There the course was administered over four quarters to a total of 287 undergraduates, who were typical of business students at the university. In each individual quarter, and over the whole period of study, there was a meaningful increase in motivation to manage. Changes occurred in all six aspects of managerial motivation.

During one of the four quarters I was able to obtain comparable measures on groups of students who did not undergo role-motivation training. As in the R & D context, the objective was to determine whether factors outside the training might account for the results. One of these groups was made up of stu-

EXHIBIT 36
*Effects of Managerial Role-Motivation Training
on the Motivation to Manage of Business Administration
Students at the University of Oregon*

Motivation to Manage	Before Course	After Course
High Motivation	145 (51%)	200 (70%)
Low Motivation	142 (49%)	87 (30%)
Favorable Attitude Toward Authority		
High Motivation	121 (42%)	143 (50%)
Low Motivation	166 (58%)	144 (50%)
Desire to Compete		
High Motivation	143 (50%)	165 (58%)
Low Motivation	144 (50%)	122 (42%)
Assertive Motivation		
High Motivation	131 (46%)	157 (55%)
Low Motivation	156 (54%)	130 (45%)
Desire to Exercise Power		
High Motivation	123 (43%)	193 (67%)
Low Motivation	164 (57%)	94 (33%)
Desire for a Distinctive Position		
High Motivation	216 (75%)	228 (79%)
Low Motivation	71 (25%)	59 (21%)
Sense of Responsibility		
High Motivation	151 (53%)	167 (58%)
Low Motivation	136 (47%)	120 (42%)

dents in a business law course. The other contained education majors enrolled in the introductory course in their field. In neither case was there any meaningful change in motivation to manage over the period of the course. Thus the changes in the students experiencing managerial role-motivation training appear to be specific to that particular development experience.

Two studies also were conducted in the business school context to determine whether the motivational impact of the training was retained. In one instance a third measurement was obtained on those who had undergone role-motivation training; this was done as long as possible after the initial training, yet while the individual still remained in the university setting. On the average this third measurement occurred 10.6 months after completion of role-motivation training. At best there was a slight drop in motivation; most of the increase in motivation to manage was retained. Such decline as did occur appears to have been almost immediate. Those students whose motivation to manage was measured well over a year after completing the course showed no more decline than those who were measured for a third time less than six months after.

The second study compared seniors, and mostly graduating seniors, who had experienced managerial role-motivation training at some time during their college education, with a simi-

---

EXHIBIT 37
Results of a Comparison Study to See If Changes
Comparable to Those With Role-Motivation Training
Occur in Other Courses

Motivation to manage...	*...as the quarter began...*	*...at the end*
Students in Managerial Role-Motivation Training		
High Motivation	23 (40%)	38 (67%)
Low Motivation	34 (60%)	19 (33%)
Students in Business Law I		
High Motivation	30 (56%)	26 (48%)
Low Motivation	24 (44%)	28 (52%)
Students in The School in American Life		
High Motivation	55 (47%)	56 (48%)
Low Motivation	61 (53%)	60 (52%)

lar group who had not. In general those who had had the managerial training experienced it about a year prior to the measurement. As far as could be ascertained, the two groups were similar in composition, and any motivational differences could not

EXHIBIT 38
Results of Studies to Determine if Changes in Motivation to Manage are Retained

Motivation to Manage	Before Role-Motivation Training	Immediately After Training	An Average of 10.6 Months After Training
High Motivation	62 (48%)	93 (72%)	91 (70%)
Low Motivation	67 (52%)	36 (28%)	38 (30%)

Motivation to Manage	Among Senior Students Finishing College *Who Had Undergone Role-Motivation Training* at Some Point (Usually as Juniors)	Among Senior Students Finishing College *Who Never Had Undergone Role-Motivation Training*
High Motivation	49 (60%)	18 (33%)
Low Motivation	33 (40%)	37 (67%)

Favorable Attitude Toward Authority		
High Motivation	41 (50%)	14 (25%)
Low Motivation	41 (50%)	41 (75%)

Assertive Motivation		
High Motivation	61 (74%)	29 (53%)
Low Motivation	21 (26%)	26 (47%)

Desire to Exercise Power		
High Motivation	42 (51%)	24 (44%)
Low Motivation	40 (49%)	31 (56%)

Sense of Responsibility		
High Motivation	51 (62%)	25 (45%)
Low Motivation	31 (38%)	30 (55%)

be attributed to differences in the number of females in each group, say, or a reason of that type. Yet there were motivational differences, and they consistently favored the trained group. The trained students ended up being more favorably disposed to authority, more assertive, more power motivated, and more responsible. Without managerial role-motivation training a business education clearly did little for motivation to manage at all; with such training a real improvement was in evidence at graduation.

Change Among Women

In discussing women as a new source of managerial talent I pointed out that there was a need for management development in this area. What I had in mind was managerial role-motivation training, and the reason for this conclusion is inherent in some of the research we have done.

The student groups that I taught at the University of Oregon were roughly 14 percent female. When analysis focuses specifically on these female students there is little to indicate any difference from the males. Role-motivation training does improve motivation to manage in the female population. Among the constituent aspects of managerial motivation, those relating to attitudes toward authority, assertive motivation, desire to exercise power, and the desire for a distinctive position improve the most among the females. The motivational changes do not dissipate immediately, but are still in evidence well after the training has been completed, just as among the males. Everything that is currently known seems to indicate that utilizing managerial role-motivation training with female managerial candidates will contribute not only to a reduction in talent shortages, but to closing the gap caused by the underrepresentation of women in managerial positions as well.

EXHIBIT 39
*Effects of Managerial Role-Motivation Training on
the Motivation to Manage of Female College Students*

Motivation to Manage	Before Course	After Course
High Motivation	18 (44%)	29 (71%)
Low Motivation	23 (56%)	12 (29%)
Favorable Attitude Toward Authority		
High Motivation	17 (41%)	25 (61%)
Low Motivation	24 (59%)	16 (39%)
Assertive Motivation		
High Motivation	24 (59%)	30 (73%)
Low Motivation	17 (41%)	11 (27%)
Desire to Exercise Power		
High Motivation	25 (61%)	31 (76%)
Low Motivation	16 (39%)	10 (24%)
Desire for a Distinctive Position		
High Motivation	25 (61%)	32 (78%)
Low Motivation	16 (39%)	9 (22%)

Those Who Change and Those Who Do Not

Not everyone increases in motivation to manage with exposure
to role-motivation training. In fact, over the period of training a
few people typically decline, although this does not occur because of the training itself. Some research was done with the
Oregon students in an effort to determine what kinds of people
benefit the most from managerial role-motivation training, and
while a great deal more needs to be learned in this regard, there
are some positive findings to report.

The major factors which have been identified as predictors

of susceptibility to change are aspects of temperament as measured by certain psychological tests. Specifically, it appears that very active people respond well to the training, while more passive individuals do not. In addition, those who are rather independent tend to increase their managerial motivation and those who are more dependent do not.

These findings make a good deal of sense. The training presents managerial work as a very active process in which the manager has to do things on his own, and in particular has to initiate action with regard to subordinates who are doing poorly. The manager is portrayed as a person who helps others rather than being helped by them. This picture may very well serve to "turn off" certain kinds of people. An individual who is basically passive and inactive, who does things only to the extent he is forced to by external events, would not be expected to become very enthused at the prospect of managing in the vein depicted. Similarly, those who prefer to lean on others for help could well be expected to find the training not very stimulating. They probably would want no part of a managerial job which called for such independent action. It stands to reason, then, that these more passive and dependent people would "tune out" certain aspects of the training as not for them, with the result that it would have less chance to stimulate their motivation to manage.

In any event, it does appear possible to select a group of people who will be maximally responsive to managerial role-motivation training if a company wishes to do so. By doing this it can maximize the return on the investment in training, because practically everyone can be expected to be affected. Whether this approach is desirable in a given situation, however, will depend on the particular circumstances involved.

Efforts have been made to identify other factors, in addition to these aspects of temperament, that might predict who will increase in motivation to manage, but without much success. For instance, whether a participant reports high satisfaction with the training does not matter at all; those who say they like it less

EXHIBIT 40

*Changes in Motivation to Manage Resulting From
Role-Motivation Training in People of
Different Temperaments*

Motivation to Manage	Decreased Motivation	Little or No Motivational Change	Increased Motivation
Active People	4 (9%)	18 (38%)	25 (53%)
Passive People	17 (15%)	58 (53%)	35 (32%)
Independent People	12 (11%)	43 (41%)	51 (48%)
Dependent People	9 (18%)	33 (64%)	9 (18%)
Favorable Attitude Toward Authority			
Active People	3 (6%)	35 (75%)	9 (19%)
Passive People	12 (11%)	81 (74%)	17 (15%)
Independent People	8 (7%)	75 (71%)	23 (22%)
Dependent People	7 (14%)	41 (80%)	3 (6%)
Desire to Compete			
Active People	7 (15%)	24 (51%)	16 (34%)
Passive People	16 (15%)	73 (66%)	21 (19%)
Independent People	15 (14%)	62 (59%)	29 (27%)
Dependent People	8 (16%)	35 (68%)	8 (16%)
Desire to Exercise Power			
Active People	4 (9%)	30 (64%)	13 (27%)
Passive People	11 (10%)	70 (64%)	29 (26%)
Independent People	6 (6%)	71 (67%)	29 (27%)
Dependent People	9 (18%)	29 (57%)	13 (25%)
Sense of Responsibility			
Active People	7 (15%)	26 (55%)	14 (30%)
Passive People	14 (13%)	71 (64%)	25 (23%)
Independent People	11 (10%)	64 (61%)	31 (29%)
Dependent People	10 (20%)	33 (64%)	8 (16%)

change as much as those who say they like it more. The same holds true for such factors as age of the participants, managerial job level, prior managerial performance effectiveness, intelligence, and college grades. On none of these factors do those who are at one end of the distribution change their motivation any more than those at the other end.

Even grades on examinations given in the specific course do not make a difference. Those who acquire the most knowledge apparently are not necessarily the ones whose motivation is affected the most.

The Feasibility of Role-Motivation Training

As an approach to reducing managerial talent shortages, role-motivation training has much to recommend it. The conventional, classroom-type context tends to be readily accepted, and the training is generally viewed as interesting by the participants. When the students at the University of Oregon were asked to grade the lectures, the average grade was 3.66 on a scale where an A was 4.0 and an F was 0. Furthermore, it does focus directly on the matter of motivation to manage when hierarchic control is used.

The studies just described were conducted prior to the advent of major changes on college campuses, and the training was all done by the author. Neither factor appears to be crucial, however. Professor Robert Bowin, of Eastern Washington State College, has just published a study in which he obtained sizable increases in managerial motivation with a group of "new generation" students that he taught in 1972. Professor Bowin's course was similar to the one I have described, but with case analyses by the students added. Professor Abraham Korman, now at the Baruch College of the City University of New York, obtained evidence of sizable changes in a group of evening students that he taught at the University of Oregon. This study is of particular interest because these individuals, many of whom were older and held fulltime jobs, started the training with higher levels of motivation to manage than any of the groups discussed previously, even the R&D managers. Yet their increase in motivation was at least equal to that in the other groups.

This is not to say that managerial role-motivation training always works. I have had reports of attempts to raise the level of motivation to manage that have failed. My own experience with the approach has been consistently positive, and others have had similar success. Yet some have not. It is not at all clear why this is, although it would appear to have something to do with the particular instructor. In any event any claim that the training can provide a universal panacea must be treated with skepticism. Under the most ideal conditions not everyone experiencing it changes, and in some cases it appears no one changes at all. Hopefully as more is learned about the approach, the instances of failure can be reduced. In the meantime, role-motivation training does appear to be sufficiently feasible to justify its use in attempting to cope with a potential dearth of competent managers.

15

Management Development and Education for Managing

The preceding chapter dealt with managerial role-motivation training only, and implicitly assumed in-house use of this procedure by an individual company. The question may be raised: Are there other people approaches that might be used? Furthermore, what about more extensive use of management development techniques outside the company — techniques that seek to change motives and attitudes in collegiate schools of business and management, for instance.

Compatible Management Development Procedures

A rather wide spectrum of management development procedures has been shown to have an impact on managers' motives, attitudes, and values. However, many of these approaches appear to yield results which at best would contribute nothing to solving the talent shortage problem and at worst would accentuate it.

I already have indicated my strong reservations about such approaches as sensitivity training, T-grouping, growth laboratories, communication laboratories, encounter sessions, and gestalt therapy. As management development techniques, these procedures are more likely to increase the gap between the demand for managers and the supply than to reduce it, at least as long as hierarchic control continues to be used. The same conclusion emerges from research on liberal arts and humanities programs such as the Bell System's program at the University of Pennsylvania.

Another broad category of management development efforts has been known for a number of years as human relations training. These programs first appeared shortly after World War II and were strongly influenced by the ideas and research related to democratic leadership emerging from the Institute for Social Research at the University of Michigan. In this period, human relations training was almost invariably synonomous with the teaching of power equalization and participative management. A study published as early as 1948 by Professor Raymond Katzell, now at New York University, dealing with the effects of human relations training on supervisors of the Illinois Central Railroad, yielded results that have been repeated many times since. There was an increased acceptance of and more favorable attitude toward democratic leadership after training.

Over the years the term human relations training has come to be applied to a much more diverse range of programs, some of which may in fact concern themselves very little with the democratic leadership theme which was the original core concept. However, there still are many human relations training programs being given which retain the early focus. Thus, a recent report by Professors Bernard Baum, of the University of Illinois at Chicago Circle, Peter Sorensen, of George William College, and William Place, of Purdue University, deals with a program which is described as "heavily human relations oriented, especially in terms of what has been defined as power equalization." They found that the program which was given in an insurance company served to move control over decisions down, so that management was perceived to exercise less control and the clerical staff more. In essence the training taught the managers they should abdicate their power and authority, and they did. Training of this kind will not decrease the gap between demand for effective managers and the supply; in fact it may increase it, to the extent hierarchic control is retained in the existing structure.

Programs of the sensitivity training, humanities, and pure human relations types, if given with managerial role-motivation training, might well be expected to have a neutralizing effect. In contrast, there are management development procedures which would appear to be entirely compatible with the role-motivation approach.

One of these is achievement motivation training of the kind described by Professors David McClelland and David Winter. In their studies they have shown that this training does have an effect on the propensity to undertake entrepreneurial ventures. One such study conducted in India demonstrated the value of this approach as an aid to economic development. When the two-year periods before and after training were contrasted, a dramatic increase in entrepreneurial activity was in evidence in the trained group of managers. A similar group which did not experience the training maintained a constant level of entrepreneurial activity over the four-year period. Furthermore, the highest rate of entrepreneurial effort occurred among those trained managers who were in charge of a business and thus in the best position to institute new ventures.

There are some data indicating that these kinds of gains from achievement motivation training may also be obtainable in the corporate setting. A study conducted by J. Aronoff and George Litwin, of Harvard University, indicated that in one company a group of managers who underwent achievement training were more successful in the ensuing two years than a comparable group who went through a regular management-development program.

Other types of management development efforts may also be highly compatible with managerial role-motivation training. Any procedure which would serve to reduce the pervasive disturbance in authority relationships that appears to be engulfing our society would be of particular value. Managerial role-motivation training does seem to contribute to this goal, but there may be other equally or even more effective techniques. Similarly, whatever steps can be taken to reduce the closely related guilt at assuming a position of authority should be taken. Management development efforts which will contribute to increased availability of the necessary will to manage must make the participants at least comfortable in the role of manager, and hopefully happy in it. This should be the ultimate objective of any people-oriented approach to change that is designed to deal with the managerial talent problem.

EXHIBIT 41

Extent to Which Managers in India Were Active in Stimulating Business Growth and New Business Ventures (Entrepreneurship) as Related to Achievement Motivation Training

Managerial Group	Over a Two-Year Period Before Achievement Training	Over a Two-year Period After Achievement Training
46 managers who received training and were in charge of a business	26	67
30 managers who received training but were not in charge of a business	3	30
73 managers who did not receive training	22	25

Percent Entrepreneurially Active

Adapted from the book *Motivating Economic Achievement* by David C. McClelland and David G. Winter.

Training Strategies

In-house management development is an entirely feasible procedure when there are a number of managers at the same location who need training. Under such circumstances one can easily initiate efforts of the kind represented by managerial role-motivation training by releasing the manager for training a few hours each week or by conducting the training sessions after hours. Disruption of regular duties is minimal and the training is spread over a considerable period of time in a manner which at least to date has proved desirable.

This approach is not applicable, however, when the group to be trained is widely dispersed geographically, and it is not feasible in the small company which has relatively few managers to train in any event. Solutions in these instances have typically involved the use of such expedients as a company-operated school for executives, a university-sponsored executive development program, or regular business school courses that give degree credit. More recently there has been some use of individualized self-instruction employing combined audio and video procedures.

To the extent that these approaches involve intensive, very short-term programs removed from the work environment, they probably lose some of their capacity to produce motivational change. However, there is little evidence on this point, and certainly some such changes have been demonstrated after concentrated programs of this type. In any event, the approach is somewhat disruptive to regular work performance and tends to be quite expensive.

The use of self-instructional procedures made possible by the new technology offers some exciting prospects. It is still too early to know whether such approaches can produce motivational and attitude changes, however. We are working on some procedures for adapting managerial role-motivation training to movie film and other visual media, and ultimately we will study the change potential of these adaptations. But at the moment no results of this type of study are available.

The Role of the Business School

An obvious solution to many of these problems and uncertainties is for programs related to managerial role-motivation training to be absorbed into the standard curricula of the nation's business schools. This approach would have the added advantage that sizable numbers of individuals in the society would experience increased motivation to manage, many of them at a relatively early age. The possibility of having some real impact, either slowing the present decline or even reversing it, does exist here because of the large numbers involved. It is in fact the failure of the business schools to inculcate a will to manage that leads Harvard Professor J. Sterling Livingston to chastise them in his widely cited article "Myth of the Well-Educated Manager."

Yet several considerations, both practical and ethical, indicate the need for caution. All-out advocacy of the widespread use of role-motivation approaches is not justified on the basis of the existing data.

One problem is posed by the fact that most business schools take as their primary task the inculcation of knowledge related to business operations. This knowledge is applicable in many contexts, however. Thus, in 1972, roughly 3.7 percent of M.B.A. graduates went to work for the Federal Government and 2.7 percent were employed in education. Furthermore, a large number go into professional organizations. In 1972, 11.3 percent of the M.B.A.'s went into public accounting and 4.2 percent into management consulting. An unknown number go into very small companies or start their own small businesses. Many become professionals, specialists, or career salesmen. All this adds up to the fact that most business schools, at both the undergraduate and graduate levels, are preparing their students for a sizable range of occupations and careers — not just to manage in business corporations.

In many of these careers, motivation to manage has no value at all, and in some of them it may even be harmful. As previously noted, managerial motivation has very little relevance in professional organizations. We did not find it related to consulting success, nor to success as a salesman or as a university professor. It also is apparently less important in many small organizations where everything is done on a strictly face-to-face basis and few managers are needed. In companies of much fewer than 300 employees it is probably not very important at all.

One study I conducted with research scientists in an industrial setting indicated a negative relationship between motivation to manage and research success. This single finding would not be worth taking too seriously were it not for the fact that a more recent study, by Benjamin Gantz, Clara Erickson, and Robert Stephensen, at the China Lake, California, Naval Weapons Center, on a much larger group of scientists produced essentially comparable results. The implication is that by developing managerial motivation in an individual it is entirely possible that we would be harming his chances for success in creative areas such as scientific research.

Given findings like these, it seems to me indefensible on either practical or ethical grounds to initiate widespread, compulsory managerial role-motivation training in the business schools. Such training is fine for those who are in school to learn to become managers. It is at best wasteful, and at worst actually harmful, for the rather large and presumably increasing number who are there for some other purpose.

An additional question regarding the feasibility of basing a revival of the will to manage in the business schools as they are currently organized stems from findings regarding the motivation to manage of university professors of business.

Certainly enthusiasm for managing is not high in the group as a whole. Based on my data, less than 20 percent of the professors studied have motivation to manage equal to that of the average manager; many are very low. This may well be a desirable state of affairs insofar as scholarship and research is concerned, but it does not suggest an environment in which faculty members can be expected to stimulate a real love of managing in their students.

I do not mean to say that the business schools do not serve a useful purpose in society; they do, especially in the creation and transmission of knowledge regarding business. But as currently operated they are not an effective primary source of developed *managerial* talent.

A School of Managing

What appear to be needed are either separate schools or separate components of existing schools which focus specifically and exclusively on developing managers. These schools would utilize motives and attitudes as much as intelligence and prior knowledge (grade point average) in selecting their students. They would leave no question that their primary objective is to train highly successful managers, so that students who did not want this role could avoid it by not applying. They would attempt to build on an existing base of motivation to manage, developing it further, and adding such knowledge as a series of job analyses of existing management positions might recommend. To the extent possible, features of managerial role-motivation training would be built into all courses. In my opinion, such schools should operate primarily at the undergraduate level so as to get their students out into the real world of managing at as early an age as possible.

Teachers would be selected in terms of their ability to contribute to the schools' objectives. This would require some enthusiasm and respect for the role of manager as well as a solid foundation of knowledge in some area that managers need. Managerial experience would certainly be desirable, but only successful and satisfying managerial experience.

There is no reason why such a school of managing could not be developed as a subsidiary of many existing business schools. To maintain its mission, however, I believe it would have to operate as a separate and distinct entity with its own procedures, courses, and faculty. In some universities this might pose a problem, given the restraints imposed by faculty organization and administrative tradition. In other universities it should be a viable approach. An alternative would be the creation of separate schools of managing, presumably with funding from private sources. The latter approach may well appear increasingly attractive to many large corporations as the talent crunch becomes increasingly evident.

In any event, I believe effectively organized and operated schools of managing can make a sizable contribution to solving the problem of managerial talent shortages.

16

The Crunch Reconsidered

Given the variety of approaches that a company can take to prevent a substantial managerial manpower shortage, there seems to be a good chance that, as a result of collective action, the crunch in managerial talent will be avoided. Whether or not this turns out to be the case depends entirely on whether companies do the necessary planning and what action they take on the basis of these plans.

The Components of a Strategy

Among the short-run techniques that companies can use for coping with a lack of managerial talent is flexible retirement, which retains the services of effective managers for as long as possible. Another is accelerated recruiting of those known to possess the will to manage. Both approaches can serve to buy time to implement strategies with a long-term payoff.

Which of the various alternatives of a long-term nature is selected to cope with the problem will depend on the situation of the particular company. Differences in internal and external labor force characteristics, geographical location, core technology, market requirements, and the like may indicate that a strategy which is ideal for one firm is totally infeasible for another.

For example, whether or not an input strategy emphasizing new sources of talent is appropriate depends in large part on the availability of particular groups of people in the existing labor market. Groups which are currently underrepresented in the ranks of management and which could provide new sources of managerial talent include women, minorities, less well-educated employees, and foreign nationals. While it is unlikely that a reliance on only one of these sources would provide a sufficient amount of managerial talent, it is possible that a comprehensive effort designed to tap all possible new sources could satisfy existing needs. On the other hand the effectiveness of this approach inevitably is contingent on the number of companies which utilize it. Given the current governmental pressures with regard to fair employment practices, there is a high probability that a great many firms will opt for the new sources strategy. Thus, even if a company does choose to rely primarily on new sources of managerial talent, it would do well to implement other approaches as well.

Two major classes of mediator approaches that appear to offer real promise as strategies for assuring needed managerial manpower are organization planning and management development. Within the framework of organization planning a company might resort to some type of variable structuring which relies on sources of control other than the hierarchic, and which substitutes other motives which are in greater supply for the deficient motivation to manage. Whether this is possible depends to a considerable degree on the nature of the company's workforce and of the tasks to be performed.

Within the management development context, procedures such as managerial role-motivation training can be used to stimulate the will to manage. The use of this approach is much less likely to be constrained by existing circumstances than either utilizing new talent sources or variable structuring. For this reason the management development strategy has considerable appeal. However, it may face one difficulty not considered previously. In a society where the will to manage is on the wane, a point may be reached at which even getting people into training programs designed to make them effective managers may prove difficult.

As in other situations where supply does not equal demand, the ultimate solution to the problem of getting young men and women into training programs is likely to come in the form of money. Increased compensation levels alone do not appear to offer a meaningful solution to the talent shortage problem, however. No doubt very high salaries would attract a large number of individuals to managerial work, but they would be people motivated primarily by a desire for money and not by a desire to manage. From what is currently known it seems certain that all that would be accomplished by escalating salary levels is that a large number of incompetent managers would be added to the payroll.

However, increased compensation levels combined with appropriate management development and/or education for managing should present a very different picture. In this situation the money serves as an inducement not only to take a managerial position, but also to enter into a change process aimed at making a person truly want to manage. Thus it seems likely, and appropriate, that executive compensation levels should rise at an accelerated rate in the years to come. Hopefully this will occur not as an outgrowth of an all-out talent war among the large corporations, but as part of a broad-based effort to induce young people to develop motivation to manage.

The Problem for Society

The discussion of what can be done about managerial manpower shortages has been largely from the viewpoint of the organizations affected, because it seems to me realistically that that is where solutions to the immediate problem will be found. However, it is important to ask how a society could get itself into this situation, and what might be done outside the organizational context at the level of the individual, the family, and the society as a whole.

Chapter 7 contains my admittedly speculative conclusions regarding the sources of the change we are experiencing. I do not feel that government is likely to be very helpful in dealing with these matters, and perhaps it should not be. A key requirement for a successful society is that it be highly differentiated in its membership, so that there are a great many different kinds of people suited to the great variety of tasks that must be performed. One of the problems of the increasing ease of mass communication is that it can serve as a homogenizing force by influencing child-rearing practices as well as attitudes and values so that they coalesce closely around a common core. As a result, needed motives such as the will to manage, which never were overly abundant, may tend toward outright extinction. It is not at all clear to me how government could or should serve effectively to restore the needed differentiation.

On the other hand individuals and families can, if they will. What we as a society appear to need currently as much as anything else is a degree of tolerance and understanding for those who assume the needed authority roles. Exercising authority can be personally rewarding, but it also has many built-in stresses. If we continue to treat those who are willing to face these stresses the way we have been over the past ten years, it will not be long before no one wants the top jobs — at least no one who can perform in them effectively. It takes a very strong will to manage to take a position and retain it when a major concomitant of the position is the antagonism of a large number of the people with whom one must work. Yet this is exactly the situation that exists in many sectors of this country today. The problem is epitomized in the presidency; our recent presidents have left office either through assassination or as bitter and demoralized individuals. Mistakes which in a prior time, with more positive attitudes toward authority, would have been easily tolerated are no longer tolerated in an age which is antiauthority; positive accomplishments weigh very little in the balance.

The problem insofar as leadership in our society is concerned is compounded by an additional factor. Not only will many persons who might otherwise desire to manage avoid doing so because of the antagonism they anticipate, but many who express antagonism will be similarly constrained from managing by the internal dynamics of their emotions.

People who are in constant opposition to existing authority tend to avoid positions of authority. If they are forced into such positions, they avoid exercising the control expected of them, and thus appear ineffective. The problem is one of guilt. Hating those people who have exercised authority over them, they come to hate themselves when they see themselves doing, or anticipate doing, the same things. Thus the sword of intolerance is two-edged. It keeps those who cannot tolerate authority from assuming managerial positions and it makes exercising authority so unpleasant for others that they too avoid managing. Ultimately, if something is not done to reverse the trend, a society which has become strongly antagonistic to authority faces the prospect of devolving into a state of leaderlessness, where no one wants to exercise authority, to lead, or to control. The result is anarchy. The United States does appear to face such a prospect.

Society's Solutions

Historically, changes in the authority relationships characterizing a society have emanated from the family and the ways in which parents and children act and feel toward each other. Changes of this kind require a long lead time, because the children affected must grow to maturity before changed child-rearing practices can have a meaningful impact on the society's functioning. This is why I have stressed more immediate solutions involving actions that companies and other organizations can take to secure sufficient numbers of competent managers. If we wait and rely on traditional processes of social change it may well be too late, at least for America as we now know it.

Yet I do not intend that we should ignore these traditional processes in the family and in the educational system. They are important and the sooner changes can be initiated there, the better off society will be in the long run. Assuming a continuing need for hierarchic control (and we are currently far from having developed social mechanisms that might fully and efficiently replace that need), action by individuals and families, in addition to organizations, seems essential. The company strategies I have considered have the potential for solving the immediate problems of a managerial talent shortage, but they will do nothing to create a social milieu in which managing effectively is highly valued, and in which those who exercise authority are typically treated with respect and understanding, or even tolerance.

For that purpose, reliance must be placed on developments in the home and at school. To the extent parents, both mothers and fathers, are able to present models of the effective, tempered, yet satisfying use of authority to their children, it seems likely that these children will develop in ways that provide both an adequate supply of motivation to manage and a social environment that nurtures it. This assumes that teachers and others in the school system provide equally effective authority models as children go out of the home and have their first experiences with hierarchic control in an organizational context. Both in the family and in the school there must be an end to the kind of abdication and repudiation of authority roles which serves not only to produce a state of *laissez-faire* in intergenerational relationships, but to seriously disrupt the transmission of society's values.

Publications Discussed

Allen, Louis A. "The T-Group: Short Cut or Short Circuit." *Business Horizons*, August 1973, pp. 53-64.

Aronoff, J., and Litwin, G. H. "Achievement Motivation Training and Executive Advancement." *Journal of Applied Behavioral Science*, 1971, pp. 215-229.

Athanassiades, John C. "The Distortion of Upward Communication in Hierarchical Organizations." *Academy of Management Journal*, 1973, pp. 207-226.

Barnett, Rosalind C., and Tagiuri, Renato. "What Young People Think About Managers." *Harvard Business Review*, May 1973, pp. 106-118.

Barton, Allen H. "The Columbia Crisis: Campus, Vietnam, and the Ghetto." *Public Opinion Quarterly*, 1968, pp. 333-351.

Baum, Bernard H.; Sorensen, Peter F.; and Place, William S. "The Effect of Managerial Training on Organizational Control: An Experimental Study." *Organizational Behavior and Human Performance*, 1970, pp. 170-182.

Beer, Michael. "The Technology of Organization Development." In *Handbook of Industrial and Organizational Psychology*, edited by Marvin D. Dunnette. Chicago: Rand McNally and Co., 1974.

Benham, Thomas W. "What Are the People Thinking?" *Personnel Administrator*, March 1972, pp. 17-18.

Bentz, V. Jon. "The Sears Experience in the Investigation, Description, and Prediction of Executive Behavior." In *Measuring Executive Effectiveness*, edited by Frederic R. Wickert and Dalton E. McFarland, pp. 147-205. New York: Appleton-Century Crofts, 1967.

Berkwitt, George J. "The Crisis in Management Talent." *Dun's*, February 1973, pp. 56-58.

Blake, Robert R., and Mouton, Jane Srygley. *Building a Dynamic Corporation Through Grid Organization Development*. Reading, Mass.: Addison-Wesley Publishing Co., 1969.

Blankenship, L. Vaughn, and Miles, Raymond E. "Organizational Structure and Managerial Decision Behavior." *Administrative Science Quarterly*, 1968, pp. 106-120.

Block, Jeanne H.; Haan, Norma; and Smith, M. Brewster. "Activism and Apathy in Contemporary Adolescents." In *Understanding Adolescence — Current Developments in Adolescent Psychology*, edited by James F. Adams, pp. 198-231. Boston: Allyn and Bacon, 1968.

Bower, Marvin. *The Will to Manage*. New York: McGraw-Hill Book Co., 1966.

Bowin, Robert Bruce. "Attitude Change Toward a Theory of Managerial Motivation." *Academy of Management Journal*, 1973, pp. 686-691.

Braunstein, Daniel N., and Haines, George H. "Student Stereotypes of Business." *Business Horizons*, February 1971, pp. 73-80.

Bray, Douglas W., and Grant, Donald L. "The Assessment Center in the Measurement of Potential for Business Management." *Psychological Monographs*, No. 625 (1966).

Brenner, Marshall H. "Management Development for Women." *Personnel Journal*, March 1972, pp. 165-169.

Bureau of National Affairs, Inc. "ASPA-BNA Survey: Management and the Generation Gap." *Bulletin to Management,* December 1969.

————. "Women and Minorities in Management and in Personnel Management." *Personnel Policies Forum,* December 1971.

Campbell, John P.; Dunnette, Marvin D.; Lawler, Edward E.; and Weick, Karl E. *Managerial Behavior, Performance, and Effectiveness.* New York: McGraw-Hill Book Co., 1970.

Carroll, Stephen J., and Tosi, Henry L. *Management By Objectives: Applications and Research.* New York: The Macmillan Co., 1973.

Carruth, Eleanore. "The Legal Explosion Has Left Business Shell-Shocked." *Fortune,* April 1973, pp.65-69 and 155-157.

Collins, Orvis F., and Moore, David G. *The Enterprising Man.* East Lansing, Mich.: Bureau of Business and Economic Research, Michigan State University, 1964.

Cowan, Gloria. "The Changing Values of Youth." *Personnel Administration,* November 1971, pp. 21-27.

Dawson, Leslie M. "Campus Attitudes Toward Business." *MSU Business Topics,* Summer 1969, pp. 36-46.

Deep, Samuel D.; Bass, Bernard M; and Vaughan, James A. "Some Effects on Business Gaming of Previous Quasi-T Group Affiliations." *Journal of Applied Psychology,* 1967, pp. 426-431.

DeSalvia, Donald N., and Gemmill, Gary R. "An Exploratory Study of the Personal Value Systems of College Students and Managers." *Academy of Management Journal,* 1971, pp. 227-238.

Dewey, John. *Democracy and Education: An Introduction to the Philosophy of Education.* New York: The Macmillan Co., 1916.

Evans, Martin T. "Managing the New Managers." *Personnel Administration,* May 1971, pp. 31-38.

Faltermayer, Edmund. "Youth After the Revolution." *Fortune,* March 1973, pp. 145-158.

Flacks, Richard. "Who Protests: The Social Bases of the Student Movement." In *Protest: Student Activism in America,* edited by

Julian Foster and Durwood Long, pp. 134-157. New York: William Morrow and Co., 1970.

Ford, Robert N. *Motivation Through the Work Itself.* New York: American Management Association, 1969.

Freedman, Mervin B., and Kanzer, Paul. "Psychology of a Strike." In *Student Activism and Protest,* edited by Edward E. Sampson and Harold A. Korn, pp. 142-157. San Francisco: Jossey-Bass, 1970.

French, Wendell L., and Bell, Cecil H. *Organization Development: Behavioral Science Interventions for Organization Improvement.* Englewood Cliffs, N. J.: Prentice-Hall, 1973.

Friedlander, Frank, and Brown, L. Dave. "Organization Development." In *Annual Review of Psychology,* pp. 313-341. Palo Alto: Annual Reviews, 1974.

Galbraith, Jay. *Designing Complex Organizations.* Reading, Mass.: Addison-Wesley Publishing Co., 1973.

Gantz, Benjamin S.; Erickson, Clara O.; and Stephenson, Robert W. "Measuring the Motivation to Manage in a Research and Development Population." *American Psychological Association Proceedings,* 1971, pp. 129-130.

———. "Some Determinants of Promotion in a Research and Development Population." *American Psychological Association Proceedings,* 1972, pp. 451-452.

Ghiselli, Edwin E. *The Validity of Occupational Aptitude Tests.* New York: John Wiley and Sons, 1966.

———. *Explorations in Managerial Talent.* Pacific Palisades, Calif.: Goodyear Publishing Company, 1971.

Golembiewski, Robert T. *Renewing Organizations: The Laboratory Approach to Planned Change.* Itasca, Ill: F. E. Peacock Publishers, 1972.

Gooding, Judson. "The Accelerated Generation Moves Into Management." *Fortune,* March 1971, pp. 101-104 and 115-118.

Goodstadt, Barry, and Kipnis, David. "Situational Influences on the Use of Power." *Journal of Applied Psychology,* 1970, pp. 201-207.

Hadden, Jeffrey K. "The Private Generation." *Psychology Today*, October 1969, pp. 32-35 and 68-69.

Hayghe, Howard. "Labor Force Activity of Married Women." *Monthly Labor Review*, April 1973, pp. 31-36.

Hertz, David B. *New Power for Management: Computer Systems and Management Science.* New York: McGraw-Hill Book Co., 1969.

Hicks, Robert L. "Developing the Top Management Group in a Total Systems Organization." *Personnel Journal*, 1971, pp. 675-682.

Hlavacek, James D., and Thompson, Victor A. "Bureaucracy and New Product Innovation." *Academy of Management Journal*, 1973, pp. 361-372.

Horowitz, Irving L., and Friedland, William H. *The Knowledge Factory: Student Power and Academic Politics in America.* Chicago: Aldine Publishing Co., 1970.

Katzell, Raymond A. "Testing a Training Program in Human Relations." *Personnel Psychology*, 1948, pp. 319-329.

Keniston, Kenneth. "Sources of Student Dissent." In *Student Activism and Protest*, edited by Edward E. Sampson and Harold A. Korn, pp. 158-190. San Francisco: Jossey-Bass, 1970.

Kerpelman, Larry C. *Activists and Nonactivists: A Psychological Study of American College Students.* New York: Behavioral Publications, 1972.

Korman, Abraham K. "Some Interrelationships Between Measures of Managerial Behavior." Unpublished manuscript.

———. *Industrial and Organizational Psychology.* Englewood Cliffs, N. J.: Prentice-Hall, 1971.

Krishnan, Rama. "Democratic Participation in Decision-Making by Employees in American Corporations." *Academy of Management Journal*, 1974, pp. 339-347.

Lacey, Lynn A. "Discriminability of the Miner Sentence Completion Scale Among Supervisory and Non-Supervisory Scientists and Engineers." *Academy of Management Journal*, 1974, pp. 354-358.

Leavitt, Harold J. "Applied Organizational Change in Industry: Structural, Technological, and Humanistic Approaches." In *Handbook of Organizations,* edited by James G. March, pp. 1144-1170. Chicago: Rand McNally and Co., 1965.

Leavitt, Harold J., and Whisler, Thomas L. "Management in the 1980s." *Harvard Business Review,* November 1958, pp. 41-48.

Lecht, Leonard A. *Manpower Needs for National Goals in the 1970s.* New York: Praeger Publishers, 1969.

Lee, Hak Chong. "Human Resources Administration: In the Computer Age." In *Human Resources Administration: Problems of Growth and Change,* edited by William J. Wasmuth, *et al.,* pp. 323-426. Boston: Houghton Mifflin Co., 1970.

Lehman, I.J., and Hill, W.H. *Michigan State University 1958 and 1967 Freshmen: A Contrast in Profiles.* East Lansing: Office of Evaluation Services, Michigan State University, 1969.

Lipset, Seymour M. *Student Politics.* New York: Basic Books, 1967.

Lipset, Seymour M., and Ladd, Everett C. ". . . and What Professors Think." *Psychology Today,* November 1970, pp. 49-51 and 106.

Lipset, Seymour M., and Schaflander, Gerald M. *Passion and Politics: Student Activism in America.* Boston: Little, Brown and Co., 1971.

Livingston, J. Sterling. "Myth of the Well-Educated Manager." *Harvard Business Review,* January 1971, pp. 79-89.

Lowin, Aaron, and Craig, James R. "Influence of Level of Performance on Managerial Style: An Experimental Object-Lesson in the Ambiguity of Correlational Data." *Organizational Behavior and Human Performance,* 1968, pp. 440-458.

Lubell, Samuel. "Where the New Left Dissidents Come From." *Boston Globe,* 10 October 1968.

Mahoney, Thomas A.; Jerdee, Thomas H.; and Nash, Allan N. *The Identification of Management Potential.* Dubuque, Iowa: William C. Brown Co., 1961.

Maliver, Bruce L. *The Encounter Game.* New York: Stein and Day

Publishers, 1973.

McClelland, David C. *The Achieving Society.* New York: D. Van Nostrand Co., 1961.

——. "Business Drive and National Achievement." *Harvard Business Review,* July 1962, pp. 99-112.

McClelland, David C., and Winter, David G. *Motivating Economic Achievement.* New York: The Free Press, 1969.

Morris, Charles and Small, Linwood. "Changes in Conceptions of the Good Life by American College Students from 1950 to 1970." *Journal of Personality and Social Psychology,* 1971, pp. 254-260.

Mulder, Mauk, and Wilke, Henk. "Participation and Power Equalization." *Organizational Behavior and Human Performance,* 1970, pp. 430-448.

Ondrack, Daniel A. "Attitudes Toward Authority." *Personnel Administration,* May 1971, pp. 8-17.

——. "Emerging Occupational Values: A Review and Some Findings." *Academy of Management Journal,* 1973, pp. 423-432.

Patten, Thomas H. *OD — Emerging Dimensions and Concepts.* American Society for Training and Development, 1973.

Patton, Arch. "The Coming Scramble for Executive Talent." *Harvard Business Review,* May 1967, pp. 155-171.

Pelz, Donald C., and Andrews, Frank M. *Scientists in Organizations: Productive Climates for Research and Development.* New York: John Wiley and Sons, 1966.

Perham, John C. "The Companies That Build Executive Talent." *Dun's,* May 1973, pp. 51-55.

Peterson, Richard E. *The Scope of Organized Student Protest in 1967-68.* Princeton, N.J.: Educational Testing Service, 1968.

Powell, Reed M., and Schlacter, John L. "Participative Management — A Panacea?" *Academy of Management Journal,* June 1971, pp. 165-173.

Powell, Reed M., and Stinson, John E. "The Worth of Laboratory Training." *Business Horizons,* August 1971, pp. 87-95.

Prentice-Hall, Inc. "Business and the New Breed Employee."

P-H Personnel Management: Policies and Practices, 1971.

Reeser, Clayton. "Some Potential Human Problems of the Project Form of Organization." *Academy of Management Journal*, 1969, pp. 459-467.

Rotter, Julian B. "Generalized Expectancies for Interpersonal Trust." *American Psychologist*, 1971, pp. 443-452.

————. "External Control and Internal Control." *Psychology Today*, June 1971, pp. 37-42 and 58-59.

Sashkin, Marshall, and Maier, Norman R. F. "Sex Effects in Delegation." *Personnel Psychology*, 1971, pp. 471-476.

Schein, Virginia Ellen. "The Relationship Between Sex Role Stereotypes and Requisite Management Characteristics." *Journal of Applied Psychology*, 1973, pp. 95-100.

Schwartz, Eleanor B. *The Sex Barrier in Business*. Atlanta: Bureau of Business and Economic Research, Georgia State University, 1971.

Silver, Allan. "Who Cares for Columbia?" *New York Review of Books*, January 1969, pp. 15-19 and 22-24.

Spock, Benjamin M. *Baby and Child Care*. New York: Pocket Books, 1946.

Steiner, George A., and Ryan, William G. *Industrial Project Management*. New York: The Macmillan Co., 1968.

Swart, J. Carroll. "The Worth of Humanistic Management: Some Contemporary Examples." *Business Horizons*, June 1973, pp. 41-50.

Tannenbaum, Arnold S. *Control in Organizations*. New York: McGraw-Hill Book Co., 1968.

Tarnowieski, Dale. *The Changing Success Ethic*. New York: American Management Association, 1973.

Travis, Sophia C. "The U. S. Labor Force: Projections to 1985." *Monthly Labor Review*, May 1970, pp. 3-12.

Vetter, Eric W. *Manpower Planning for High Talent Personnel*. Ann Arbor: Bureau of Industrial Relations, University of Michigan, 1967.

Viteles, Morris S. "Human Relations and the Humanities in the

Education of Business Leaders: Evaluation of a Program of Humanistic Studies for Executives." *Personnel Psychology,* 1959, pp. 1-28.

Ward, Lewis B., and Athos, Anthony G. *Student Expectations of Corporate Life: Implications for Management Recruiting.* Boston: Graduate School of Business Administration, Harvard University, 1972.

Watts, William A., and Whittaker, David. "Free Speech Advocates at Berkeley." *Journal of Applied Behavioral Science,*1966, pp. 41-62.

Whisler, Thomas L. *The Impact of Computers on Organizations.* New York: Praeger Publishers, 1970.

Wilcox, Herbert G. "Hierarchy, Human Nature, and the Participative Panacea." *Public Administration Review,* 1969, pp. 52-63.

Wilemon, David L., and Gemmill, Gary R. "The Venture Manager as a Corporate Innovator." *California Management Review,* Fall 1973, pp. 49-56.

Wohlking, Wallace. "Attitude Change, Behavior Change: The Role of the Training Department." *California Management Review,* Winter 1970, pp. 45-50.

Yankelovich, Daniel. "What They Believe." *Fortune,* January 1969, pp. 70-71 and 179-181.

Publications by the Author Dealing in Greater Detail With the Topics Discussed

Publications Dealing Specifically With
Motivation to Manage and Its Development

"The Kuder Preference Record in Management Appraisal." *Personnel Psychology*, 1960, pp. 187-196.

"The Effects of a Course in Psychology on the Attitudes of Research and Development Supervisors." *Journal of Applied Psychology*, 1960, pp. 224-232.

"Management Development and Attitude Change." *Personnel Administration*, May 1961, pp. 21-26.

"Personality and Ability Factors in Sales Performance." *Journal of Applied Psychology*, 1962, pp. 6-13.

"Evidence Regarding the Value of a Management Course Based on Behavioral Science Subject Matter." *Journal of Business*, 1963, pp. 325-335.

The Management of Ineffective Performance. New York: McGraw-Hill Book Co., 1963.

Studies in Management Education. New York: Springer Publishing Co., 1965.

"The Prediction of Managerial and Research Success." *Personnel Administration,* September 1965, pp. 12-16.

Introduction to Industrial Clinical Psychology. New York: McGraw-Hill Book Co., 1966.

The School Administrator and Organizational Character. Eugene, Ore.: University of Oregon Press, 1967.

"The Managerial Motivation of School Administrators." *Educational Administration Quarterly,* 1968, pp. 55-71.

"Early Identification of Managerial Talent." *Personnel and Guidance Journal,* 1968, pp. 586-591.

"Managerial Talent Among Undergraduate and Graduate Business Students." *Personnel and Guidance Journal,* 1969, pp. 995-1,000 (with Norman R. Smith).

"Management Development and Its Ethical Limitations." *The Federal Accountant,* September 1969, pp. 54-62.

"Personality Tests as Predictors of Consulting Success." *Personnel Psychology,* 1971, pp. 191-204.

"Changes in Student Attitudes Toward Bureaucratic Role Prescriptions During the 1960s." *Administrative Science Quarterly,* 1971, pp. 351-364.

"Personnel Attitudes and Motivation." *Annual Review of Psychology,* 1973, pp. 379-402 (with H. Peter Dachler).

"The Management Consulting Firm as a Source of High-Level Managerial Talent." *Academy of Management Journal,* 1973, pp. 253-264.

"The Real Crunch in Managerial Manpower." *Harvard Business Review,* November 1973, pp. 146-158.

"The OD-Management Development Conflict." *Business Horizons,* November 1973, pp. 31-36.

"Role Motivation Theory of Managerial Effectiveness in Simulated Organizations of Varying Degrees of Structure." *Journal of Applied Psychology,* 1974, pp. 31-37 (with John R. Rizzo, Dorothy N. Harlow, and James W. Hill).

"Motivation to Manage Among Women: Studies of Business Managers and Educational Administrators. *"Journal of Vocational Behavior,* 1974.

"Motivation to Manage Among Women: Studies of College Students." *Journal of Vocational Behavior,* 1974.

"Student Attitudes Toward Bureaucratic Role Prescriptions and Prospects for Managerial Talent Shortages." *Personnel Psychology,* 1974.

"The Management of Ineffective Performance." In *Handbook of Industrial and Organizational Psychology,* edited by Marvin D. Dunnette. Chicago: Rand McNally and Co., 1974 (with J. Frank Brewer).

Publications Focusing on Topics Other Than Motivation to Manage

"Some Aspects of the Executive Personality." *Journal of Applied Psychology,* 1955, pp. 348-353 (with John E. Culver).

Intelligence in the United States. Westport, Conn: Greenwood Press, 1973.

"On the Use of a Short Vocabulary Test to Measure General Intelligence." *Journal of Educational Psychology,* 1961, pp. 157-160.

"Bridging the Gulf in Organizational Performance." *Harvard Business Review,* July 1968, pp. 102-110.

"An Input-Output Model for Personnel Strategies." *Business Horizons,* May 1969, pp. 71-78.

Personal Psychology. New York: The Macmillan Co., 1969.

Management Theory. New York: The Macmillan Co., 1971.

The Management Process: Theory, Research, and Practice. New York: The Macmillan Co., 1973.

Personnel and Industrial Relations: A Managerial Approach. New York: The Macmillan Co., 1973 (with Mary Green Miner).

A Guide to Personnel Management. Washington, D.C.: BNA Books, 1973 (with Mary Green Miner).

"Personnel Strategies in the Small Business Organization." *Journal of Small Business Management*, 1973, pp. 13-16.

"Psychological Testing and Fair Employment Practices: A Testing Program That Does Not Discriminate." *Personnel Psychology*, 1974, pp. 49-62.

Index

A

Achievement motivation 113-115, 211-214
—training for 235-236
Activism, student 49-54, 91-105, 116, 119-121
Allen, Louis 197
American Management Association 87
American Society for Personnel Administration 87
American Telephone & Telegraph Co. 141, 187, 206 (See also Bell System)
Andrews, Frank 171
Antioch 94
Appraisal, management 22-27, 131-133
Army and Air Force Exchange Service 161
Aronoff, J. 235
Assertive motivation, as a component of motivation to manage 8t, 39t, 41, 41t, 42t, 43, 51t, 53, 56t, 57t, 60t, 62t, 63, 65t, 66t, 74t, 103t, 146t, 148t, 223t, 225t, 227t
Assertiveness, among student activists 96
Athanassiades, John 207
Athos, Anthony 76-78, 86, 88
Atlanta University 152
Attitude surveys 78-81
Attitude toward authority (See Authority)
Attitudes of college students toward business 80-84

Authoritarianism, studies on 73-75
Authority, changing attitude toward 73-79, 88-90, 246-248
Authority, favorable attitude toward, as a component of motivation to manage 8t, 39t, 51t, 53, 56t, 57t, 60t, 62t, 63, 65t, 66t, 67, 74t, 75, 103t, 146t, 148t, 220t, 223t, 225t, 227t, 229t
Authority relationships 94-95, 108-121, 236

B

Ball State University 173
Barnett, Rosalind 81, 147
Barton, Allen 98
Baruch College 230
Bass, Bernard 196
Baum, Bernard 234
Beer, Michael 190, 195
Bell, Cecil 191
Bell System 198, 234 (See also American Telephone & Telegraph Co.)
Benham, Thomas 81
Bentz, Jon 141
Berkwitt, George 7
Black managers 151-154
Blake, Robert 188-190, 194
Blankenship, Vaughn 162
Block, Jeanne 94-95
Bower, Marvin 13-14, 32
Bowin, Robert 230
Braunstein, Daniel 82, 88
Bray, Douglas 141

Brenner, Marshall 149
Brown, L. Dave 188, 193, 195
Bureau of National Affairs, Inc.,
The 87, 143, 151, 152
Business, attitudes toward
81-84
Business schools, 88, 233
—blacks in 152
—female students in 145
—role of 238-240
Business school students, studies of
motivation to manage of
33-69, 99-101, 145-148, 222-226

C

Campbell, John 141
Career choice of college students
35-40
Career preference of high school
students 82, 83*t*
Carroll, Stephen 177
Carruth, Eleanore 181
Case Western Reserve University
188
Center for Creative Leadership
84
Centralization in decision making,
pressures for 180-183
Change
—among college students
49-105
—in the labor force 4
—in motivation to manage
218-230
—in organizations 159-241
—social 107-121, 245-248
China Lake Naval Weapons Center
32, 239
City University of New York
152-153, 230
Civil rights movement 92
College students, studies of
33-105, 222-226
Collins, Orvis 211
Columbia University 97-98, 119,
152

Communication in organizations
207-208
Company characteristics preferred
by business students 84-86
Competitive motivation, as a component of motivation to manage
8*t*, 36, 36*t*, 39*t*, 41, 45*t*, 46, 51*t*, 53,
56*t*, 57*t*, 59-60, 60*t*, 61, 62*t*, 63, 65*t*,
66*t*, 74*t*, 103*t*, 133, 146*t*, 148*t*, 220*t*,
223*t*, 229*t*
Computerized information systems
207-208
Computers, effect of on management 159-168, 180-181
Consultants, management 31,
41-43, 208-209
Control, in individuals, studies of
71-73
Control, in organizations
170-172, 196-197, 201-214, 248
Cornell University 219
Corning Glass Works 190
Corporate model, ideal stra-
tegic 189, 194-196
Cowan, Gloria 170
Craig, James 178
Culver, John 141

D

Dawson, Leslie 81
D. B. A. students 37-40
Decision making
—centralization of 180-183
—effect of computers on
161-166
Decisions, participative 178-180
Deep, Samuel 196
Democratic leadership 234
Department store managers
23-26
—female 144-145, 146*t*
DeSalvia, Donald 83
Dewey, John 119
Discrimination in employment
151-153, 181-182
Distinctive position, desire for, as a
component of motivation to man-

age   9*t*, 38, 39*t*, 40-41, 45*t*, 46, 51*t*, 54, 56*t*, 57*t*, 59-60, 60*t*, 65*t*, 66*t*, 65-67, 74*t*, 98, 144*t*, 146*t*, 148*t*, 223*t*, 227*t*
Dunnette, Marvin   141
Dun's   7, 10

E

Eastern Washington State College 230
Educational systems, and societal values   114, 248
Educational Testing Service   93
Encounter techniques in organization development   197
Entrepreneurs   113, 211-214, 235-236
Equal Employment Opportunity Commission   181
Erickson, Clara   84, 239
Evans, Martin   90
Exxon   10, 141

F

Fair employment practices   153, 181-182
Faltermayer, Edmund   79
Family relationships and societal values   114-121, 247-248
Federal Communications Commission   181
Flacks, Richard   120
Ford, Robert   206
Foreign nationals, as a source of managerial talent   156-157
Fortune   78-81, 87, 181
Freedman, Mervin   73
French, Wendell   191
Friedland, William   96
Friedlander, Frank   187, 193, 195

G

Galbraith, Jay   210
Gantz, Benjamin   84, 239

Gemmill, Gary   83, 213
General Electric   10
George William College   234
Georgia State University   143, 207
Ghiselli, Edwin   140
Golembiewski, Robert   191, 194
Gooding, Judson   87
Goodstadt, Barry   178
Government managers   64-67
Graduate students in business 37-40, 59-61
Grant, Donald   141
Group control in organizations 172, 196-197, 203-205, 210-211, 213-214
Guilt, feelings of in authority relationships   109-113, 118, 236, 247
Gulf and Western   10

H

Haan, Norma   94-95
Hadden, Jeffrey   79
Haines, George   82, 88
Harvard Business Review   82, 147, 173
Harvard Business School   76-78, 81, 84, 147
Harvard University   92, 113, 152, 235, 238
Harwood Manufacturing Company 176
Hayghe, Howard   117
Hertz, David   162
Hicks, Robert   161
Hierarchic control in organizations 201-214, 248
High school students, career preference of   82
Hill, W. H.   75
Hlavecek, James   213
Horowitz, Irving   96
Human relations training   234
Humanism   111

I

IBM   10
Illinois Central Railroad   234
Indiana University   209
Institute for Social Research
   171, 234
Intelligence, among blacks   152
Intelligence, and managerial success   140-142
Iowa State University   178
ITT   10

J

Jerdee, Thomas   140
Job enlargement/enrichment
   206
Job knowledge, and managerial success   141-142
Job satisfaction, participative management and   175-176
Johnson & Johnson   10

K

Kanzer, Paul   73
Katzell, Raymond   234
Keniston, Kenneth   118
Kerpelman, Larry   95
Kipnis, David   178
Korman, Abraham   152-153, 230
Krishnan, Rama   173

L

Labor force, the changing   4
Laboratory, T-group, or sensitivity training   188-199, 233-235
Lacey, Lynn   32
Ladd, Everett   99
Laissez-faire leadership style
   170-171, 197, 204-205, 209, 248
Lawler, Edward   141
Lawsuits against companies
   181-183
Leadership style
—democratic   234
—*laissez-faire*   170-171, 197, 204-205, 209, 248
—participative   169-185
Leavitt, Harold   159, 161, 215
Lecht, Leonard   6
Lee, Hak Chong   162
Lehman, I. J.   75
Liberal arts students   57-59, 101
Lipset, Seymour   92, 99
Litwin, George   235
Livingston, J. Sterling   238
Lowin, Aaron   178
Lubell, Samuel   97

M

Mahoney, Thomas   140
Maier, Norman   147
Maliver, Dr. Bruce   197
Management appraisal   22-27, 131-132
Management by objectives (MBO)
   177, 189
Management consultants   31, 41-43, 208-209
Management Development Corporation (MDC)   43-46
Management development programs   23-24, 215-241
Management, participative   112, 169-185, 234
Management potential, aspects of   140-142
Managerial motivation (See Motivation to manage)
Managerial role-motivation training   215-241
Managerial talent, coming shortage of   3-11, 243-248
—and college students   67-69, 86
—and managerial role-motivation training   230-231
—and manpower planning   125-135
—and new sources of   137-157

—and participative management 183-185
—and schools of managing   241
—and the New Left   104-105
—and variable organization structuring   213-214
—effect of computers on 159-162
Managers
—department store   23-26
—female   144-150
—government   64-67
—marketing   29-31
—older   134-135
—R&D   22-23, 28-31, 218-222
—younger   63-69, 87-88, 167
Managers and students, motivation to manage compared   61-64
Managing, education for   233-241
Manpower planning, managerial 125-135
Marketing managers   29-31
Matrix structures in organizations 208-211
M.B.A. students   37-40, 59-61, 238
McClellend, David   113-115, 212, 235
McKinsey & Company   3, 13, 162
Metropolitan Life Insurance Company   148
Michigan State University   75, 81, 177, 189
Middle management, effect of computers on   161-163
Miles, Raymond   162
Minority employees and discrimination in employment 181-182
Minority-group members as managers   150-154
Moore, David   211
Morris, Charles   76
Motivation, achievement   113-115, 211-214, 235-236
Motivation to manage

—and achievement motivation 114
—aspects of   14-18
—of blacks   151-152
—and career choice   36*t*
—of college students   33-69, 74-75, 91-105, 222-226
—components of   8-9*t*
—decline in   4-5, 7-11, 108
—lack of   19-22
—of management consultants 41-43
—and managerial success   13-32
—and organization structure 201-214
—and participative management 184-185
—training programs for   215-241
—of university professors   40-41
—and wanting to be a manager 33-47
—of women   144-150
Mouton, Jane   188-190, 194
Mulder, Mauk   179

N

Nash, Allan   140
National Planning Association   6
New Left, the   53, 91, 104-105
New York State School of Industrial and Labor Relations   219
New York University   169, 234
Norton Company   10

O

Ohio State University   176, 196
Oil company managers   22-23, 28-31, 218-222
Older managers   134-135
Ondrack, Daniel   73, 76
Opinion Research Corporation 81
Organization development (OD) 187-199
Organization planning   160

268 / *Index*

Organization renewal   194
Organization structure   160,
163-167, 201-214
Organizations preferred by high
school students   82, 83*t*

P

Participative management   112,
169-185, 234
Participatory   democracy
169-170, 183
Patten, Thomas   189
Patton, Arch   3-7
Peabody University   72
Pelz, Donald   171
People, effecting change in
159-160, 215-241
Performance appraisal (See Ap-
praisal)
Performance, employee
—and participative management
175-178
—ineffective   216-217
Perham, John   10
Permissiveness,   parental
117-120
Peterson, Richard   93, 99
Place, William   234
Portland State University   50,
63, 103
Powell, Reed   176, 196
Power, desire to exercise, as a com-
ponent of motivation to manage
9*t*, 39*t*, 42*t*, 43, 51*t*, 54-56, 56*t*, 57*t*,
58, 59, 60*t*, 65*t*, 66*t*, 74*t*, 98, 144*t*,
146*t*, 148*t*, 220*t*, 223*t*, 225*t*, 227*t*,
229*t*
Power equalization   170, 234
Power motivation, among student
activists   98
Prentice-Hall   87
Productivity
—and organization development
198
—and participative management
175-176

Professional business firms
133-134
Professional control in organiza-
tions   171-172,   202-203,
210-211, 214
Professors, university   40-41,
239-240
Project management   208-211
Protest , student   91-105
Psychology Today   78-79
Purdue University   234

R

R & D managers   22-23, 28-31,
218-222
Recruiting of managerial candidates
137-139
Reeser, Clayton   209
Research scientists   239
Retirement policies   134-135
Revlon   10
Role-motivation   training
215-231
Roles, sex   8*t*, 53, 96
Rotter, Julian   71-73, 76, 109
Rutgers University   96
Ryan, William   209

S

San Francisco State College   73
Sashkin, Marshall   147
Schein, Virginia   148
Schlacter, John   176
School administrators   26-27,
64-67
Schools of business (See Business
schools)
Schwartz, Eleanor   143
Scientific Methods, Inc.   188
Sears, Roebuck   141
Self-actualization   90
Self-perceptions, student   77*t*
Sense of responsibility, among stu-
dent activists   96
Sense of responsibility for routine
matters, as a component of moti-

vation to manage   9t, 39t, 45t, 46, 51t, 54-55, 56t, 57t, 60t, 62t, 63, 65t, 66t, 74t, 103t, 146t, 148t, 220t, 223t, 225t, 229t
Sensitivity training   188-199, 233-235
Silver, Allan   97
Small businesses   133-134
Small, Linwood   76
Smith, Brewster   94-95
Societal values
—changes in   75
—problems of   245-248
—roots of change in   107-121
—transmission of   115-119
Sorenson, Peter   234
Spock, Dr. Benjamin   119
Standard Oil of New Jersey   141
Stanford University   159
State employment service managers   64-67
State University of New York at Albany   162, 213
State University of New York at Buffalo   162
Steiner, George   209
Stephenson, Robert   84, 239
Stinson, John   196
Strategies for preventing managerial talent shortages   130-135
Structure, organization   159-160, 163-167, 201-214
Student activism   49-54, 91-105, 116
Student activists, family backgrounds of   119-121
Student attitudes, surveys of   98
Student power   98
Students (See College, High school)
Students for a Democratic Society   92
Success, managerial   13-32
Swart, Carroll   173
Swarthmore   94
Syracuse University   83, 213

T

Tagiuri, Renato   81, 147
Tannenbaum, Arnold   171
Tarnowieski, Dale   87
Task control in organizations   172, 205-206, 211-214
Technological change in organizations   159-168
Temple University   178
Textron   10
Thompson, Victor   213
Tosi, Henry   177
Training programs
—achievement   motivation   235-236
—human relations   234
—laboratory, T-group, or sensitivity   188-199, 233-235
—managerial   role   motiation   215-241
Training strategies   237-238
Travis, Sophia   5
Trust, studies of   71-73
Tulane University   4

U

University of California at Berkeley   51, 92, 94, 98, 99, 120, 140, 162
University of California at Los Angeles (UCLA)   209
University of California at Santa Cruz   96
University of Chicago   120, 152, 161
University of Connecticut   71-73
University of Florida   76, 213
University of Georgia   191
University of Hawaii   209
University of Illinois at Chicago Circle   234
University of Maryland   50, 56-59, 75, 101, 103, 177
University of Massachusetts   73, 95
University of Michigan   76, 147, 171, 234

University of Minnesota, Industrial Relations Center 140
University of Nevada 52
University of Oregon 49-52, 55-56, 59, 61, 67, 101, 103, 222, 226-227, 230
University of Pennsylvania 198, 234
University of Pittsburgh 196
University of Rochester 82
University of South Florida 50, 52, 61
University of Southern California 149
University of Toronto 73, 76, 90
University of Washington 191
Upgrading programs 154
U. S. Bureau of Labor Statistics 117
Utrecht University 179

V

Values
—of organization development 190-194
—societal (See Societal values)
Variable structuring of organizations 202-206
Vaughn, James 196
Venture teams 211-214
Vetter, Eric 4
Vietnam War 93, 97
Viteles, Morris 198

W

Ward, Lewis 76-78, 86, 88
Watts, William 99
Wayne State University 170
Weick, Karl 141
Western Kentucky University 178
Western Michigan University 43, 46, 50
Whisler, Thomas 161, 165
Whittaker, David 99
Wilcox, Herbert 169
Wilemon, David 213
Wilke, Henk 179
Will to manage 14 (See also Motivation to manage)
Will to Manage, The 13
Winter, David 235
Wohlking, Wallace 219
Women
—as managers 143-150, 226-227
—discrimination in employment of 181-182
—employment of 116-117
Women's liberation movement 116, 149

Y

Yale University 118
Yankelovich, Daniel 78
Younger generation 68, 193-194
Younger managers 63-69, 87-88, 167
Youngstown State University 173